Beverly Waugh Bond, Thomas Osmond Summers

The Positive Evidences of Christianity

Beverly Waugh Bond, Thomas Osmond Summers

The Positive Evidences of Christianity

ISBN/EAN: 9783337166885

Printed in Europe, USA, Canada, Australia, Japan

Cover: Foto ©Lupo / pixelio.de

More available books at **www.hansebooks.com**

THE POSITIVE
Evidences of Christianity.

BY

THE REV. B. W. BOND,

Of the Baltimore Conference, M. E. Church, South.

EDITED BY THOS. O. SUMMERS, D.D., LL.D.

Nashville, Tenn.:
SOUTHERN METHODIST PUBLISHING HOUSE.
1880.

Entered, according to Act of Congress, in the year 1880, by
B. W. BOND,
in the Office of the Librarian of Congress, at Washington.

INTRODUCTORY NOTE.

THE author of this vigorous treatise is an estimable minister of the Baltimore Conference of the Methodist Episcopal Church, South. He bears the honored name of Beverly Waugh, late Bishop in the M. E. Church—a warm and life-long friend of the *Bond* connection, in Maryland, to which the author belongs. It may well be supposed, therefore, that he was steeped in Methodism from his birth; and if Methodism is "Christianity in earnest," as Dr. Chalmers says, an earnest defense of Christianity may be expected in this work. The reader will not be disappointed.

The conception of the book originated in the author's careful perusal and study of the best works on the Evidences of Christianity—Paley, of course, being prominent. Encouraged by judicious friends, he prosecuted his investigations, and committed his views to writing, until they were developed into a well-proportioned treatise of sufficient size, and, we will add, of due importance, to justify its publication. We have had the pleasure and profit of its perusal as it has been passing through the press, and we hesitate not to say it is an excellent *résumé* of the Evidences of Christianity, as presented by Paley, Row, and other apologists, embodying much fresh original matter adapted to the "perilous times" in which we live. Some, perhaps, may think that it was hardly necessary to refute for the thousandth time the argument of Hume against the possibility of proving a miracle—as, *e. g.*, the resurrection of Christ, on which the system of Christianity is based—especially as Hume virtually acknowledged its worthlessness to Campbell, who *graveled* him, as he says he "*graveled*" a Jesuit in the Jesuits'

College of La Flèche, where he used his argument to expose the fiction of popish miracles—"perhaps you may think," he writes to Campbell, "the sophistry of it savors plainly of the place of its birth." Indeed, it does! But, contemptible as it may be thought, and oft-refuted as it has been, it is continually paraded by unbelievers, and must be continually exposed by those who are set for the defense of the gospel.

The Reverend Doctor Abbott, preaching in Oxford University, makes a fling at Paley's Evidences and Horæ Paulinæ—and with good reason—as, following in the wake of Hume, he eliminates every thing miraculous from the Gospel History, except a few cases of healing, which he would say are no more miracles than those wrought at the tomb of the Abbé Paris—that is, they were the effects of imagination, etc., and not supernatural works at all.

Truly, it behooves us to contend earnestly for the faith, when it is thus assailed in the foremost Christian university of the world!

Whatever value may be assigned to the internal evidences of Christianity—and there is much, and it is fully admitted by the author of this book—yet he has done a good work in developing from the present advanced position of the science of apologetics the historical proofs of the divine original of our holy religion, demonstrating, as he has done in this treatise, that we have not followed cunningly-devised fables, and we are not deceived, nor are we deceiving others, when we affirm that *the religion of Jesus* is not of men, but is from heaven. Every believer in Christ is warranted in exclaiming, with the utmost confidence—

> Hence, and forever, from my heart
> I bid my doubts and fears depart;
> And to those hands my soul resign,
> Which bear credentials so divine.

THOS. O. SUMMERS.

Nashville, Tenn., April 13, 1880.

CONTENTS.

PART FIRST.

The Competency and the Credibility of the Evidence.

CHAPTER I.
Necessity of Evidence—Plan of the Work, . . 9

CHAPTER II.
The Possibility of Miracles, ... 13

CHAPTER III.
The Competency of the Evidence—I. The Competency of Evidence in General to Prove Miracles, ... 29

CHAPTER IV.
The Competency of the Evidence—II. Probable Evidence is Sufficient to Prove a Revelation, ... 59

CHAPTER V.

The Authenticity of the Evidence, ... **75**

PART SECOND.
The Weight of the Evidence—The Superhuman Facts.

CHAPTER I.
The Superhuman Advent of Christ, . . . **111**

CHAPTER II.
The Superhuman Character of Christ, . . . **128**

CHAPTER III.
The Superhuman Teaching of Christ—I. Its Reasonableness, ... **143**

CHAPTER IV.
The Superhuman Teaching of Christ—II. The Analogy of Nature—III. Its Superiority Both to Human Reason and Nature, . . **162**

CHAPTER V.
The Evidence of Prophecy, ... **194**

CHAPTER VI.

The Evidence of Miracles—I. In General, . 209

CHAPTER VII.

The Evidence of Miracles—II. The Resurrection of Christ, ... 231

CHAPTER VIII.

The Supernatural Results, ... 254

CHAPTER IX.

The Weight of the Evidence—Recapitulation and Conclusion, ... 273

The Positive Evidences of Christianity.

PART FIRST.
The Competency and the Credibility of the Evidence.

CHAPTER I.

NECESSITY OF EVIDENCE—PLAN OF THE WORK.

THE object of the following work is to prove the divinity of the Christian religion. To do this, the writer will endeavor to present simply the positive evidences that exist therefor, and to show by them that Christianity manifests a character that is plainly no less than divine. Confining the discussion strictly to this one particular, all examination into kindred questions, however interesting and closely related, should be omitted; but in the determination of the subject itself, under consideration, no pains ought to be spared to examine it in all its parts, and to apply every possible test to ascertain the truth. Rather, it should be the grateful duty of a believer to strive to show how the Christian religion, in every possible way.—as well in the great facts upon which it is founded, its own essential nature, its attendant circumstances, as in its actual results upon the characters and lives of men—exhibits such supereminent characteristics as prove it to be divine.

In this effort, however, no attempt should be made to appeal to any other principles than those that usually determine the decisions of men. Christianity does not, and cannot, claim any exemption from the application of the ordinary tests that are used to ascertain the truth of things. In matters of religion, no more than in any other human affairs, is it to be allowed that questions shall be decided by partiality, prejudice, or passion; but only upon a fair consideration, conducted according to the principles which are universally acknowledged to constitute the proper test of truth. Only by proving her claims can Religion have any authority over us, or be entitled to our reverence. To her evidences, then, must she first appeal; and in so doing, it is manifest, she must submit to be tried by the ordinary principles of evidence. Now, those principles are most distinctly and familiarly asserted and applied in the determination of trials before our ordinary courts of law. As used there, they have long been known and acknowledged as the settled maxims which the wisdom and experience of ages have agreed to be the just criterion of truth. To them, accordingly, we shall appeal; and, fearing nothing for Christianity in their application to her evidences, ask only that the reader will consent also to abide by their decision, and acquiesce in its result.

The following pages, therefore, will discuss the Christian Evidences in an order modeled upon that which is constantly followed in our legal tribunals. There the examination of the evidence presented consists of two main parts; and the inquiry is made — first, whether the testimony offered is actual testimony in the case under consideration—that is, whether it has any material bearing upon the case, and whether it is true; and, secondly, being material and true, what is its weight? Accordingly, such is the order followed here. The work is therefore divided into two Parts. The Second Part discusses—The Weight of the Evidence in favor of the Divinity of Christianity, and presents in its proof: (*a*) The Superhuman Facts upon which Christianity is founded, as displayed in—1. The Advent of Christ; 2. The Character of Christ; 3. His Teachings; 4. His Prophecies; 5. His Miracles. (*b*) Its Superhuman Results, in the changes it has wrought in the characters and lives of men, and in its wonderful growth. (*c*) The Combined Weight of these several testimonies to the one fact of the Divinity of Christianity.

Previous to this, however, we must show that the evidence thus adduced is—first, such as is proper to be brought forward in support of such a position; and, secondly, that, being in its nature proper to be adduced, it is also true. Part First, then, will be occupied with the discussion of the admissibility and genuineness of the evidence.

At the outset we are met with the objection that no testimony can be allowed to prove the supernatural, inasmuch as the occurrence in this world of any thing that is supernatural, or miraculous, is impossible in itself, and absurd. A farther objection is also made, that, even if it were possible, no testimony is competent to establish the miraculous, since our experience of nature is that it is always the same, while that of testimony is that it is sometimes false. We must, then, consider, first, the possibility of miracles; then will follow the discussion of the competency of evidence to prove them; and next, the authenticity of the evidence actually adduced, and its sufficiency to command our belief in the actual occurrence of the facts asserted by it.

CHAPTER II.

THE POSSIBILITY OF MIRACLES.

At the outset we are called upon to show that miracles are possible. The objection is urged against the divinity of Christianity that all evidence whatsoever is incompetent to establish such a claim, inasmuch as it necessarily involves the occurrence of the miraculous, and the miraculous is impossible, because the laws of nature never vary, and cannot be broken. It is said that all things earthly are linked together in one chain of physical causes and effects, in which there are no "breaks," no "rents," but in which each successive being or event has been regularly produced by the preceding being or event, through the operation of natural laws, and natural laws only, and that thus there is no room left for miracles. It is farther claimed that there exist no energies or forces except physical energies and forces, and that "matter" and "force" are the only primary and essential agencies in the world, and the sources of all the forms of being. And it is moreover urged that a miracle would be an interference with, and disturbance of, the settled order of the world, and a suspension, breaking, or abrogation of the laws of nature; and that thus, admitting even the existence of a God, who is the Author and Ruler of nature, he would be, by miracle, departing from his settled plan of procedure, in a singular and inexplicable way; that thus he would be frustrating his own laws; and finally, that thus he would show either that his original plans and laws were defective and insufficient for all his purposes, or, that being sufficient, they have been capriciously, and without adequate reason, violated by himself, and that in either case he is presented in an unworthy aspect.

1. In answering these objections against the possibility of miracles, let us first notice that we must expect, in any express and immediate revelation of God's will, something of the miraculous. Such a revelation in itself is, of necessity, miraculous; for nowhere in nature does God speak immediately to man. The very term, revelation, indicates the declaration of something unknown by nature—something made known supernaturally, or miraculously. That Christianity, therefore, which claims to be a revelation from God, should have something of the miraculous is what we ought to expect; and the fact is not therefore *a priori*,

and abstractly, an objection to the reasonableness of Christianity, but the contrary. We must *demand* of any system that professes to be by direct revelation from God, that it be miraculous. Christianity *without* it would be unreasonable, and entitled to no credit, as such a revelation.

Moreover, we must remember that these objections, if valid, destroy all hope of any revealed religion whatever. If there can be no miracle, then there can be no direct revelation from God; and so man never has had, and *never can have*, any sure hope set before him. All are like the heathen—left merely to the dim light of nature and the doubtful deduction of reason; and there never can be any sufficient light and satisfactory assurance, any clear hope. It is, then, not in the interests of Christianity only that it is necessary to establish the possibility of miracles, but also in those of all revealed religion whatsoever.

Against such objections stands the general belief of mankind, in all ages, that miracles are possible. That such is the common belief of men, appears undeniably from universal history. No people in any age have been without faith in a supernatural Power, as well as in the ability of that Power to manifest himself supernaturally to men. To men generally, it has seemed, as to Rothe, quoted by Van Oosterzee (Dogmatics, etc.), that since "God has subjected to man the powers of nature, he never could have subjected to them himself—his freedom, his almighty will—and so place in them a barrier to his own free working." To the common judgment of mankind, then, the idea has nothing absurd in it, but is thought to be agreeable with true reason. This is certainly a presumption in its favor. Any opinion in which we find the voices of the whole human race, of all ages, uniting, is surely entitled to great weight, if not to be justly regarded as the expression of the most certain conclusions attainable by human reason.

In reply, it may be urged that this opinion of the mass of mankind is denied by some men of great powers of mind and attainments, on the authority of science, and that therefore such a belief cannot be true. To this we reply: First, we should remember that scientific men, however deservedly respected, are not to be regarded as infallible. They have made many mistakes, and have changed, and changed again, many of their theories and deductions, within the memory of even one generation. The French Academy, one of the leading bodies of scientific men in the world, rejected, at various times, in the name of science (*vide* Christlieb's "Modern Doubts," etc.), (1) the use of quinine; (2) vaccination; (3) lightning-conductors; (4) the existence of meteors; (5) the steam-engine. Scientific men are yet fallible in their *deductions* as to what is and what is not *possible*. They are, also, like other men—liable to be moved by prejudice and passion, and are certainly *capable*, through their very hostility to Christianity, whenever they have such a hostility, of arriving at wrong conclusions respecting matters affecting our religion. But, secondly, miracles are not thus denied by all scientific men, nor by many of the greatest, but, on the contrary—as we shall see from extracts subsequently quoted—are asserted by them to have occurred, as shown by the inevitable deductions of science itself. The settled conclusions of science, then, cannot be said to oppose this universal conviction of mankind; nay, her teachings are claimed to be in harmony therewith. At most, her expounders are divided—at best, they are not infallible; and therefore the presumption in favor of miracles, arising from the general consent of men, remains unimpaired, to add its force to our argument.

2. But to reply more directly to those objections, it is denied that miracles are so out

of harmony with the laws of nature. Nature is not a system consisting of the working of laws admitting of no exception and no interference, nor is it of an uninterrupted chain of physical causes and effects. On the contrary, there are exceptions and interferences, and there are "rents" and "breaks" where no preceding merely physical cause can be shown, or even conceived, and where therefore we must conclude that there has been a supernatural interference—where we can only say, "This is the finger of God." For,

(1) The laws of nature—understanding that phrase in the sense in which it is commonly employed—are not invariable and without exception. The fact that water becomes lighter when frozen, in contradiction to the general law that liquids become heavier when frozen, proves there may be exceptions to general laws, and such as are caused only, so far as we can see, by the supreme will of the Creator. We know from this that God has not chosen to govern the world by one uniform and invariable law only. And, if so, it is no *more* unreasonable to conclude that he would make exceptions to such laws for the spiritual and eternal welfare of men by miracles, than he would do so for their temporary and bodily welfare, by causing water to become lighter

when frozen. And if he saw fit, and was able to make such an exception permanently for all time, in the case of some particular *substance*, as water, he could do so also in ordaining that such exceptions should likewise happen, as to all substances, at some particular *time*—as *e. g.*, the giving of a revelation.

Moreover, it is not true that the laws of nature are not interfered with. On the contrary, the lower set of laws is continually interfered with by the higher—the mechanical by the chemical, and the chemical by the vital. Thus, the force of gravitation is daily overcome by the force of the rising plant, the chemical dissolution of the body by the powers of life, etc. The heavy iron is lifted by the magnet—why may not all nature and man himself, in the presence of God, yield to the superior force of spiritual power when exerted upon them? Surely nature herself everywhere teaches the subordination, for beneficent ends, of the lower laws to the higher; and surely this, itself a higher law of nature, allows the possibility at least of the subordination of all nature in miracles, for the highest interests—the spiritual and eternal welfare—of men. At any rate, it is certain that we find that some laws of nature are continually interfered with and overcome. Miracles, then, bring no unheard-of disorder into nature. True, in miracles, the manner of their interference may be unknown, or be altogether different from that seen in nature; but the mere manner in which a thing is done cannot afford a solid ground of objection against the possibility of the thing being done. The fact remains that the laws of nature may be interfered with and overcome even by human power—it is for the objector to show why they may not also be interfered with and overcome by power that is divine.*

(2) There does not exist an uninterrupted chain of physical causes and effects. There are "rents" and "breaks," and therefore there is reason to conclude that there has been supernatural interference in nature. From the "Unseen Universe," p. 247, a work by Profs. Stewart and Tait, of England, physicists of

---

* The absurd unreasonableness of the objection against miracles is well illustrated by an incident that came under the writer's notice. A young, new-fledged son of Æsculapius, who had imbibed skeptical notions, and had read Tyndall's prayer-test arguments, was declaiming with evident great self-satisfaction against the absurdity of praying for rain, etc. "Science has demonstrated," said he, "that the falling of rain depends on atmospheric changes alone. How then can prayer bring rain? Give me a few cannon, and *I* will bring it." God is of course feebler than a scientist!

the highest authority, we take the following extract: "Formidable breaks are brought before us by science. There is, to begin with, that formidable phenomenon, the production in time of the visible universe. Secondly, there is a break hardly less formidable, the original production of life; and there is, thirdly, that break, recognized by Wallace and his school of natural history, which seems to have occurred at the first production of man. Greatly as we are indebted to Darwin, and Huxley, and those who have prominently advocated the possibility of the present 'system of things having been developed by forces and operations which we see before us, it must be regarded by us, and we think it is regarded by them, as a defect in their system, that these breaks remain unaccounted for." That the physical universe must have thus had its beginning in time, is shown also by such other scientific men of the highest authority as Sir William Thompson and Clerk Maxwell (*vide* Tait's Recent Advances in Physical Science); and the same is true also of the origin of physical life, and of the appearance of man on the earth. It thus appears that there has been no such uninterrupted "chain" of physical causes and effects as is alleged, and there is therefore no argument from this against miracles to be made in the name of science. Nay, in thus disclosing to us these "breaks," science itself teaches us that there have been miracles of the highest order; and instead of furnishing a ground for rejecting the miraculous, it affirms its existence, and even its necessity, to account for the world and its phenomena.

(3) Nor is it true that reason forces us to conclude that there are only physical agencies at work in the world. What are the *laws* of nature? The very existence of law, instead of chaos, throughout the physical universe, proves on the most reasonable supposition the existence of an all-pervading and all-governing INTELLIGENCE. In the smaller affairs of our every-day life — where we *have* personal experience — we regard the signs of order and rule as the certain marks of a controlling MIND. Must we, in those transcendent matters in which we have no experience, come to a directly opposite conclusion, when we see such signs in their utmost perfection? And what is *force*, or *energy*? The scientists themselves tell us that it is distinct from matter. All that they pretend to say about it is, that it is the working, powerful agent present in all changes occurring in matter; but what it is in itself they can tell nothing, save that it is not matter. But if it is not matter, can it be any

thing else than something that is *immaterial and spiritual*? And may it not consist merely in the working of God's will on matter just as our will, in a like incomprehensible way to us, works upon the matter of our bodies? Some of the best scientific men have concluded from the facts *of science* that there is an unseen and spiritual universe. The authors mentioned above in their remarkable book, "The Unseen Universe," elaborately argue its necessary existence from the consideration, among others, of the scientific "Principle of Continuity," "which, since this visible universe must come to an end, demands a continuance of the universe still; and thus we are forced to believe that there is something beyond that which is visible" (p. 94). And to the same conclusion they quote as follows: "The deservedly famous Dr. Thomas Young has the following passage in his lectures on natural philosophy: 'Besides this porosity, there is still room for the supposition that even the ultimate particles of matter may be permeable to the causes of attractions of various kinds, especially if those causes are immaterial; nor is there any thing in the unprejudiced study of physical philosophy that can induce us to doubt the existence of immaterial substances — on the contrary, we see analogies that lead us almost directly to such an opinion. The electrical fluid is supposed to be essentially different from common matter; the general medium of light and heat, according to some, or the principle of calorics, according to others, is equally distinct from it. We see forms of matter, differing in subtilty and mobility, under the name of solids, liquids, and gases; above these are the semi-material existences, which produce the phenomena of electricity and magnetism, and either caloric or a universal ether. Higher still, perhaps, are the causes of gravitation and the immediate agents in attractions of all kinds, which exhibit some phenomena apparently still more remote from all that is compatible with material bodies. And of these different orders of beings the more refined and immaterial appear to pervade freely the grosser. It seems therefore natural to believe that the analogy may be continued still farther, until it rises into existences absolutely immaterial and spiritual. We know not but that thousands of spiritual worlds may exist unseen forever by human eyes; nor have we any reason to suppose that even the presence of matter, in a given spot, necessarily excludes these existences from it'" (p. 201). And again, from Prof. Stokes: "Admitting to the full as highly probable, though not completely demonstrated, the applicability to living beings of the laws which have been ascertained with reference to dead matter, I feel constrained at the same time to admit the existence of a mysterious *something* lying beyond, a something *sui generis*, which I regard, not as balancing and suspending the ordinary physical laws, but as working with them, and through them, to the attainment of a desired end. What this *something*, which we call life, may be, is a profound mystery. . . . When from the phenomena of life we pass on to those of mind, we enter a region still more mysterious. We can readily imagine that we may here be dealing with phenomena altogether transcending those of mere life, in some such way as those of life transcend, as I have endeavored to infer, those of chemistry and molecular attractions, or as the laws of chemical affinity in their turn transcend those of mere mechanics. Science can be expected to do but little to aid us here, since the instrument of research is itself the object of investigation. It can but enlighten us as to the depths of our ignorance, and lead us to look to a higher aid for that which most nearly concerns our well-being" (p. 235). And the authors themselves of "The Unseen Universe," after an independent and extended discussion of the matter, say, page

221: "Let us pause for a moment, and consider the position into which science has brought us. We are led by scientific logic to an unseen, and by scientific analogy to the spirituality of this unseen. In fine, our conclusion is that the visible universe has been developed by an intelligence resident in the unseen."

(4) Farther, these facts show that miracles are not in disharmony with the history and constitution of nature, nor destructive of its order. Adopting again the language of the authors quoted above (page 21), in reference to the existence of those "breaks" which undeniably appear in nature, we may say: "If this be true, the discussion regarding miracles must be removed altogether from the domain of science, and this for the very good reason that scientific logic admits the occurrence of events at least as astounding. The question is now rather one for the historian and the moral philosopher to decide." Nay, we may claim that miracles are in analogy with some of the ordinary workings of nature. For, first, science leads us to conclude that the ordinary laws of nature are the exertions of an unseen and spiritual power, and miracles are nothing more; but, next, we cannot say that the laws of nature are *broken*, or abrogated, by miracles, but

only that they have been superseded by the coming in at a certain point of a superior cause, working not hostilely but superior to them, just as the law of gravitation is superseded—not broken, or abrogated—by me, a higher cause, when I lift a stone from the ground. In fact, the law, in such cases, *continues to operate* all the time; it is only *overcome* by the superior power present. Or else, if this be abrogation, then are the laws of nature being broken and abrogated every hour, and are not invariable; and consequently there can be no objection to miracles on that ground.

(5) Miracles, therefore, cause no destruction of the forces and laws of nature. Rather, intended, as they were in Christianity, for restoration, healing, and the bringing in again of real order and harmony, both physical and moral, to a world already disturbed by sin, they work toward the reëstablishment of the laws and forces of the real, original nature, and tend to secure her primal symmetry and strength.

(6) Finally, they do not necessarily suppose any defect in the original plans of God, to supply which defect they were afterward wrought. For we have no ground to assume that they did not form a part of his original plan, and were not intended from the first to be wrought

as occasion demanded. Rather the contrary. They were necessary in his original creations, in the beginning of the world, of physical life, and of man; they are equally necessary, as we have seen, whenever a revelation is to be given; and it is not unreasonable to infer that while their very character as miraculous precludes them from ever being common occurrences, they may be, nevertheless, if indeed they must not be, God's regular and *ordinary* method of working in the world on such *extraordinary* occasions.

We claim, then, that there appears in nature no physical or moral reason from which to conclude the impossibility of miracles; and since there is also no violence done by them to the divine attributes of truth, wisdom, and love, but, as we shall hereafter see, they are indeed most strongly prompted by all those infinite characteristics of his, we conclude that miracles are possible with God, and that therefore a revelation may be given of his will.

CHAPTER III.

THE COMPETENCY OF THE EVIDENCE—I. THE COMPETENCY OF EVIDENCE IN GENERAL TO PROVE MIRACLES.

ALLOWING, then, the possibility of miracles, our next inquiry, in the consideration of the Admissibility of the Evidence, must be whether the *character* of the evidence presented is in itself such as that it may be admitted to prove them. This will constitute our examination into the Competency of the Evidence, and will divide itself into two branches—viz.: I. The Competency of Evidence in General to Prove Miracles. II. The Sufficiency of Probable Evidence to Prove them. In the present chapter we will consider the first of these two subjects.

Christianity, indeed, alone of all religious systems, offers a recognized body of proof in support of its claims. None other, whether of the ancient mythologies or the Mohammedanism, Buddhism, etc., of the modern heathen, has ever even pretended to any evidence of its claims to be a supernatural communication of divine truth. No such body of proof as the Buddhist

Evidences, the Mohammedan Evidences, has ever been known to literature. But Christianity has always possessed and offered such an array of proof; so that the phrase, "The Christian Evidences," has become a term understood and familiar to all. Indeed, Christianity has been able to make all her advances only through those evidences. Renouncing alike the power of the sword and all appeals to passion or to prejudice; teaching, on the contrary, as one of her cardinal principles, the utmost self-sacrifice and renunciation of the world, she has constantly appealed, from the beginning, to her evidences, and sought to convince the reason of men. It was thus that she won her way— first, among the Jews; then gained, through three hundred years of persecution, gradual acceptance by the cultivated pagans of Greece and Rome; and with her evidences she next met and conquered the rude and savage barbarians, the conquerors of Rome. By them she has hitherto come off victorious from all the assaults of skepticism at home; by them she has destroyed, or is destroying, every opposing system, however gigantic, and is daily making fresh advances against the ancient and mighty systems of India and China. The history of the continual exhibition of those evidences is the record of her continual triumphs.

Subjected during a period of nearly nineteen hundred years, in the most enlightened nations and ages of the world, to the most varied and searching criticism, they still remain, not only undiminished, but immensely enlarged and strengthened, as each successive age has added, by its investigations of her proofs, and by its own test of her merits, fresh witness to her truth.

This singular exception and superiority of Christianity to all other religious systems seems of itself worthy, at once, to separate it from all others, and raise it above them all in the estimation of a candid and reflecting mind. Nay, it is not too much to claim that of itself it raises a presumption in favor of the divinity of Christianity; for were it in the power of human capacity to forge any such well-connected and elaborate evidences, it is reasonable to believe that at least one of the many founders of false systems, intellectual as they undoubtedly were, would have done so. That not one of them has, or that, having done so, the forged evidences have all been so weak as to have sunk into total oblivion, is a presumption, at least, that human capacity is not equal to the forgery of so elaborate, so complete, and so valid, a body of evidences as that which Christianity possesses. But if they have not been forged, they are genuine, and Christianity is true and divine.

The objection, however, is urged against the truth and divinity of Christianity, that all evidence whatsoever is incompetent to establish its claims. It might be supposed that it would not have been disputed by any one that it was capable, somehow, of being proved. But Christianity has been made to meet in turn every possible criticism, and accordingly it has been urged against her, among other objections, that, admitting even the possibility of miracles, yet no human testimony was sufficient to prove them, or to establish Christianity, which necessarily includes miracles. In the words of Hume, the father of this objection, it is asserted that "No testimony is sufficient to establish a miracle, since a miracle being a violation of the laws of nature, which a firm and unalterable experience has established, the proof against a miracle, from the very nature of the fact, is as entire as any argument from experience can be, whereas our experience of human veracity, which is the sole foundation of the evidence of testimony, is far from being uniform, and can therefore never preponderate against that experience which admits of no exception." In refutation of this we offer the following considerations:

1. His statement of the facts from which he draws his argument is wholly incorrect. 1st. As we have already seen, miracles are in no sense "violations of the laws of nature," any more than is every interference with the lower laws by higher powers, which we daily see—as, *e. g.*, in the overcoming by our wills of the inertia of our bodies, etc. But if these constitute "violations" of the laws of nature, then are we continually beholding them, and then our "experience," instead of establishing the inviolability of the laws of nature, in reality continually establishes the opposite. Then if the interference of a higher power with the lower laws of nature are violations of those laws, no argument drawn from our experience of the inviolability of nature can be brought against miracles; if they are not violations, then miracles, which consist essentially in such interferences, are not violations. In either case, the argument against them falls to the ground. 2d. Our "experience" of the "laws of nature" is not uniform and without exception; for that which we call the "laws of nature" is not the limited personal knowledge of the natural phenomena around him, and his deductions therefrom, which every man can have, or that any one man can possibly arrive at, but our accepted deductions from the collected observa-

tions of men generally as to all the phenomena of nature possible to be made. Nothing less than this can be called "the laws of nature." It follows that when we speak of the "experience" of those laws which men have, we cannot mean merely any and every man's knowledge of them, but human experience in general, and that too of the phenomena both of changes actually occurring under the observer's inspection, and of those things that now, remaining unchanged, yet exhibit the marks of past changes; for the laws of nature are to be deduced as well from those changes occurring in the past as from those occurring in the present. Our "experience," then, of the "laws of nature" is nothing else than our examination of all the marks that we can anywhere possibly find, by ourselves and by other men, of the mode of operation of those laws, and our comparison of those marks with our deductions as to those laws. If we find that those marks, so far as we can judge, agree with those deductions, we say that the laws of nature are uniform, and the contrary if they are not. Now, we have seen that science, which is but the body which we possess of the accepted deductions of the laws of nature, drawn as far as possible from *universal* "experience"—science itself tells us that there are "breaks" in nature where there must have been miracles. Our "experience" then of nature does admit of "exception" to her laws, and therefore no argument against miracles can be drawn from our alleged experience of their unbroken uniformity. 3d. But if this view of what we must mean by our "experience" of the laws of nature be incorrect, and we must limit that phrase to signify merely our individual experience, then it is not correct to say, in regard to the miracles narrated in the Bible, that they are *contrary* to our experience. For, in point of fact, our experience has never had any trial of them whatever, and can pronounce upon them really nothing, either favorable or unfavorable. As Paley says, "The narrative of a fact can be contrary to experience only when we or others, being present at the time and place, perceived that it did not exist; *i. e.*, when it is contrary to our own or some one else's experience of the particular fact alleged." If then we are to understand the above objection to mean that those miracles are contrary to *our* experience, the statement is plainly incorrect.

2. The facts then, supposed to support this objection, do not exist as stated by Hume, and his argument, built on them, cannot be maintained. It may, however, be said that the objection still holds, inasmuch as our experience

of the uniformity of the laws of nature teaches us the extreme improbability of miracles, and consequently the insufficiency of testimony to support them. This is an *a priori* objection, drawn, not from our experience, for we have actually no experience in the matter, but from our ideas of what is and what is not improbable; and from those ideas it receives all its weight. But what may be improbable under some, and ordinary, circumstances, may become extremely probable under other and extraordinary circumstances. A man may act in one manner in the usual circumstances of life, but entirely different in uncommon occurrences. He may be content to communicate with distant friends, in common times, for a long period, by the slower and ordinary method of a letter through the post; but on a great and pressing emergency, there may be reason enough for him to employ the extraordinary means of a telegraphic dispatch; and, then again, this having accomplished its purpose, he may relapse into his former more customary mode of communication. So God may ordinarily communicate with man only by means of the works of nature around us; but a special occasion, the demands of which the ordinary means are insufficient to meet, may lead him to communicate with us for a time, after an unusual and extraordinary manner. It will be sufficient, then, to overcome this *a priori*, or antecedent, improbability of a divine revelation drawn from our experience of the uniformity of the laws of nature, by showing, on other grounds, its great probability; and thereby, since miracles are not impossible, and since it is a general law of nature that the lower laws of nature, for wise and beneficent purposes, should suffer interference by higher powers; and since there is, for such purposes, an antecedent probability of a divine revelation, that it is therefore *a priori* probable that the usual course of nature should thus be interrupted, and miracles occur.

That such a revelation is probable, we infer from the following considerations:

1. The common opinion of men has judged it to be necessary. "That so many founders of religions should appeal to a supernatural revelation shows that nature is thought insufficient in the general opinion of men," says Butler; and this view is fully proved by the acknowledgments of the most eminent thinkers, skeptics themselves as some of them are, both of modern and of ancient times. "The ultimate fruit of all philosophy is the observation of human weakness and ignorance," says Hume. "The net results of natural theology," asserts Mill (Three Essays, etc.), "are these:

a Being of great but limited power, how or by what limited we cannot even conjecture, of great and perhaps unlimited intelligence, but perhaps also more limited than his power, who desires and pays some regard to the happiness of his creatures, but who seems to have other motives of action which he cares more for." And he finds also but little, if any, hope from the same source for the immortality of the soul. Such confessions, from the great modern leaders of skeptical thought, are surely enough to show the insufficiency of natural reason alone to give man any sure foundation for his hopes. Surely a revelation is needed to teach men the truth.*

---

* "I would disturb no man's faith," says Coleridge ("Aids to Reflection," p. 179), " in the great articles of the (falsely so called) religion of nature. But before the man rejects, and calls on other men to reject, the revelations of the gospel and the religion of Christendom, I would have him place himself in the state and under all the privations of a Simonides, when, in the fortieth day of his meditations, the sage and philosophic poet abandoned the problem in despair, only to seriously consider whether a doctrine (*i. e.*, of immortality), of the truth of which a Socrates could obtain no other assurance than what he derived from his strong wish that it should be true, and which Plato found a mystery hard to discover, and, when discovered, communicable only to the fewest of men, can, consistently with history or common sense, be classed among the articles, the belief of which is insured to all men by their mere common sense."

And this was also the conclusion of the wisest and best of the ancients. "Plato begins his discourse concerning the gods and the generation of the worlds," says Horne, "with the caution 'not to expect any thing beyond a likely conjecture concerning these things.'" Cicero, with all his vast learning, acuteness, and industry, found that he was unequal to the inquiry, and says: "If we had come into the world in such circumstances as that we could clearly and distinctly have perceived nature herself, and have been able in the course of our lives to follow her true and incorruptible directions, this alone *might* have been sufficient; but now nature has given us only some small sparks of right reason, which we so quickly extinguish with corrupt opinions and evil practices that the true light of nature nowhere appears" (Tusc. Quist. 3). And he acknowledges that "all these things are involved in deep darkness." And again, after enumerating the various opinions of philosophers as to the immortality of the soul, he concludes: "Which of these opinions is true *some god must tell us;* which is most like truth is a hard question" (*Id.*, 1). "We deny not," he says again, "that something may be true, but we deny that it can be perceived so to be, for what have we certain concerning good and evil? Nor for this are *we* to be blamed, but *nature*, which has hidden the truth in the deep" (De. Nat. Deor. Lib. 1, n. 10, 11, and Acad. Qu. Lib. 2, n. 66, 120). Now Cicero, living as he did after the great philosophers of Greece, and thoroughly versed in their writings, and being himself a man of the finest powers of mind, is well entitled to represent the sum total of the results of those, the highest, exertions of the human intellect. Accordingly Gibbon, who will not be regarded as being misled through any partiality to Christianity, shows from his writings the vanity of the speculations of philosophers in these matters of such profound interest and concern to men. He says: "The writings of Cicero represent in the most lively colors the ignorance, the errors, and the uncertainty of the ancient philosophers with regard to the immortality of the soul. When they are desirous of arming their disciples against the fear of death, they inculcate as an obvious though melancholy position, that the fatal stroke of our dissolution releases us from the calamities of life, and that those can no longer suffer who no longer exist. Yet there were a few sages of Greece and Rome who had conceived a more exalted, and, in some respects, a juster idea of human nature; though it must be confessed, that in the sublime inquiry, their reason had often been guided by their imagination, and their imagination had been prompted by their vanity. When they viewed with complacency the extent of their own mental powers, . . . and when they reflected on the desire of fame which transported them into future ages far beyond the bounds of death and the grave, they were unwilling to confound themselves with the beasts of the field, or to suppose that a being, for whose dignity they entertained the most sincere admiration, could be limited to a spot of earth and to a few years of duration. With this favorable prepossession, they summoned to their aid the science, or rather the language, of metaphysics. They soon discovered that as none of the properties of matter will apply to the operations of the mind, the human soul must consequently be a substance distinct from the body — pure, simple, and spiritual, incapable of dissolution, and susceptible of a much higher degree of virtue and happiness after the release from its corporeal prison. From these specious and noble principles the philosophers who trod in the footsteps of Plato deduced a very unjustifiable conclusion, since they asserted not only the future immortality but the past eternity of the human soul, . . . a doctrine thus removed beyond the senses and the experience of mankind might serve to amuse the leisure of a philosophic mind; or, in the silence of solitude, it might sometimes impart a ray of comfort to desponding virtue; but the faint impression which had been received in the school was soon obliterated by the commerce and business of active life. We are sufficiently acquainted with the eminent persons who flourished in the age of Cicero, and of the first Cæsars, with their actions, their characters, and their motives, to be assured that their conduct in this life was never regulated by any serious conviction of the rewards or punishments of a future state. At the bar, and in the senate of Rome, the ablest orators were not apprehensive of giving offense to their hearers by exposing that doctrine as an idle and extravagant opinion, which was rejected with contempt by every man of a liberal education and understanding.

"Since, therefore, the most sublime efforts of philosophy can extend no farther than feebly to point out the desire, the hope, or, at most, the probability, of a future state, there is nothing except a divine revelation that can ascertain the existence, and describe the condition, of the invisible country which is destined to receive the souls of men after their separation from the body."

Thus the testimony of Gibbon himself is in full support of our position. No words of ours could add to the force of this conclusion of his, in which he too not only most strongly asserts the utterly vain attempts of the highest human reason, but also remarkably declares, as the necessary inference therefrom, the absolute necessity of a divine revelation.

2. This conclusion, Horne shows (Introduction, etc.), is confirmed by the darkness and confusion existing in general among men as to the most important doctrines. Plato (*vide* Linnæus), with many other ancient philosophers, held the eternity of matter, and Aristotle the eternity of the present world, both in matter and form. The Magians believed that there are two eternal principles—the one good, the other evil. Brahminism denies the individuality of the human soul, as also many of the Greek philosophers, together with the modern pantheists, and teaches that it is a part of God, and hence that all it does is right, and the greatest crime nothing but God's act. The immortality of the soul was considered very doubtful; transmigration was taught by some; reäbsorption into the divine essence is believed in by Buddhists; Pliny says "the soul and body have no more sense after death than before we were born;" Cæsar: "Beyond death

there is place neither for care nor joy." "The Hindoos believe in one God—so completely abstracted, however, in his own essence that in this state he is emphatically the 'Unknown,' and consequently the object neither of hope nor fear; he is even destitute of intelligence, and remains in a state of profound repose. . . To him, however, the Hindoos erect no altars. The objects of their adoration commence with the triad—Brahma, Vishnu, and Siva—which represent the almighty powers of Creation, Preservation, and *Destruction*. As to the providence of God, the Epicureans held that 'what was blessed and immortal gave neither any trouble to itself nor to others;' Aristotle, that God resides in the celestial sphere, and observes nothing, and cares for nothing, beyond himself; Plato, that 'God, *fortune, and opportunity*, govern all the affairs of men' (De Legg., book 4); and polytheism allowed one god to be against men because another was favorable to them; farther, the Spartans, by law, allowed adultery in certain cases, and Plutarch, in his Life of Lycurgus, commends it. Plato says, 'He may lie who knows how to do it in a fit season,' and, with the Stoics, made a Jesuitical distinction between lying with the lips and in the mind; while Menander says, 'A lie is better than a hurtful truth.'"

3. This need of a divine revelation is farther shown by the corruptness of the morals which has always prevailed wherever the Bible has been unknown, and the utter incapacity of heathen philosophy or religion to restrain it. "Do you think," exclaims Cicero, speaking of the ancient philosophers and their teachings, "that these things had any influence upon the men, a few only excepted, who thought, and wrote, and disputed, about them? Who is there of all the philosophers whose mind, life, and manners, were conformable to right reason? Who ever made his philosophy the law and rule of his life, and not a mere show of his wit and parts? Who observed his own instructions, and lived in obedience to his own precepts?* On the contrary, many of them were slaves to filthy lusts, many to pride, many to covetousness" (Tusc. Quist. 2).

But not only was this the case as to the philosophers of Greece and Rome, and their followers — the sad helplessness into which the

---

* Who, indeed, ever did but Jesus Christ? The whole of this is a most important witness to his vast superiority to all others of the wisest of mankind. He taught by far the most sublime standard of virtue, and yet so perfectly exemplified it, under the most trying circumstances, in his character and life, that not one of his many enemies, throughout eighteen centuries, has ever been able to point out the smallest stain on his spotless robe of righteousness.

human family were plunged is even more strikingly shown by the effect of their religious systems. "For you may imagine," writes Bacon ("Essays on Unity in Religion"), "what kind of faith theirs was, when the chief doctors and fathers of their Church were the poets." Accordingly, as Horne again shows (Intro., Vol. I., Ch. 1, 5), in all the heathen world, in all ages, there have prevailed not only the greatest uncertainty, frequent absurdities, and much incompleteness, but also, in every system, something mean, selfish, or sensual. Among the ancient heathens the worship of one God was unknown. There were deities that presided over every distinct nation, city, town, grove, river, and fountain. Temples and fanes were erected to all the passions, diseases, fears, and evils, to which mankind were subject. Accordingly these divinities were—some vindictive and sanguinary; others jealous, wrathful, or deceitful; most unchaste, adulterous, and incestuous. Thus their rites were often absurd, licentious, and cruel. Prostitution was systematically annexed to various pagan temples, and in some countries was even made compulsory upon the females; and other impurities were solemnly practiced in their temples and in public, at the very thought of which our minds revolt. Numbers of men were killed in the bloody sports instituted in honor of their deities, and human sacrifices, including tender infants, were in some countries offered to propitiate them. With few exceptions, they never taught the duty of loving our enemies and forgiving injuries, but that revenge was lawful and commendable. Suicide was regarded as the strongest mark of heroism; theft was permitted both in Egypt and Sparta; abortion was allowed by Aristotle in certain cases, and the exposure of infants by Plato. Among the Romans, masters might put their slaves to death at pleasure; for the relief of the poor and destitute no provision was made; common swearing was committed by their best moralists—as, *e. g.*, Socrates, Plato, and Seneca; and the unlawful gratification of the sensual appetites was openly taught and allowed; and even in those particulars in which the best and wisest of their philosophers did teach good principles, they were forced to complain that they found the understandings of men so dark and beclouded, their wills so biased and inclined to evil, their passions so outrageous and rebellious—in short, human nature so strangely corrupted and diseased by some cause of which they were ignorant, that they could not effect any great change in the characters and lives of any considerable number of men.

If we turn from ancient to modern heathendom, we see a spectacle no less melancholy. Among savage tribes the most abject idolatry, in the worship of the heavenly bodies, animals, serpents, and dumb idols, everywhere prevail, as also sorcery and magic; while polygamy, divorce, and infanticide, together with the practice of the grossest vices, are universal. Among the most enlightened of modern heathen nations we find it much the same. In China all ranks, from the emperor downward, are full of absurd superstitions, and worship gods celestial, terrestrial, and subterraneous—gods of the hills, the valleys, the shop, and the kitchen. Altars are erected on the hills and in the groves, and idols are set up at the corners of the streets, on the sides of the road, on the banks of canals, and in the boats. Astrology, divination, and necromancy, everywhere prevail. The worship of dead ancestors is widely prevalent. In accordance with their religion, their general character is well known to be that of fraud, lying, and hypocrisy. Polygamy also universally exists, as well as the practice of exposing infants, thousands of whom die annually from this cause. In India the polytheism of the Hindoos is of the grossest kind, not fewer than three hundred and thirty million deities claiming adoration. Rites the most impure, penances the most toilsome, almost innumerable modes of self-torture, the burning or burying of widows, infanticide, submersion of the sick and the dying in the Ganges, self-immolation — these and such like are the horrid practices of their idolatry. Nor is the case much different among the Mohammedans. Fierceness, rapacity, cruelty, polygamy, and falsehood, mark their character.

Such has ever been and still is the condition of all nations without Christianity. To such a state has man ever come without a revelation. It cannot be argued that it was for the lack of intellectual ability that these nations fell into such corruptions. Some of them were most successful in all other intellectual exertions, and have never been surpassed, if ever equaled, in producing great works of art and literature, or of achieving distinction in politics or war. No; it was not because their intellects were inferior, but only because, at its best, the mind of man is incapable of forming any adequate system of religion, that Plato and Aristotle, with all the rest of the Greeks and Romans, produced such imperfect and insufficient schemes. This truth is still farther shown by the speculations of modern skeptical philosophers, who, nevertheless, have enjoyed the advantages of the knowledge of the truth revealed to us by the Scriptures. Those speculations are often contradictory and discordant among themselves, and no less also with true reason and common sense. Bolingbroke taught that all morality was resolvable into self-love, and that ambition, sensuality, and avarice, may be lawfully gratified if they may be safely gratified. Hume maintained that self-denial and humility are not virtues, but useless and mischievous; that adultery *must* be practiced if men would obtain all the advantages of life, and that if it were generally practiced it would in time cease to be scandalous, and by degrees be thought to be no crime. Both Voltaire and Helvetius advocated the most unlimited gratification of the sensual appetites; and Rousseau, according to his own printed "Confessions," was a debauched profligate, who made his feelings the only standard of right. "All that I *feel* to be right is right," he says; "whatever I *feel* to be wrong is wrong." And what the character of the French Revolution was under the direction of men entertaining similar opinions, let history tell as a witness of what men form for themselves when left to themselves. And it would be with us and our nation as with Greece and Rome, as with China, and India, and with infidel France, were we deprived of Christianity; for we are, by nature, no better than they. Thus we behold our need of a revelation from God.

4. Farther, such need must ever continue. From the very nature of the case man is unable to discover fully, by the light of nature, what he needs. (1) *Vide* "Watson's Institutes." The quality of moral actions must be presumed to be matter of revelation from God. Creation implies government, government implies law, and law must be given by revelation. This may be through nature, or through nature and direct revelation also. The latter alone is sufficient, since, 1st. There are many duties not clearly taught by nature alone. For instance, temperance is not taught, except it be by the loss of health, etc.; and therefore we should suppose that it was not required of those whose health, etc., is not injured thereby, and therefore we should have one rule for one class and another rule for another. And so, likewise, with justice, since injustice goes often unpunished in this life; and with benevolence, since nature is full of rigor. Besides, there is nothing to show us that it is our duty to worship God, nor that he may be approached in prayer, nor that there is a future state of rewards and punishments, nor, clearly, that man is immortal, nor that

there is any pardon for sin. 2d. But even were nature sufficient, our reason is insufficient; for, at the best, reason is very imperfect. Again, men's reasons greatly differ, and hence there would be diverse rules. Again, men are not sufficiently contemplative, nor sufficiently honest, for such inquiries. And still farther, if the truth were once found, and intellectual men appointed to teach it, it would yet lack the authority of a divine revelation, and so be powerless. (2) *Vide* "Wayland's Moral Science." Conscience is imperfect. 1st. Unassisted, it does not discover many obligations man is under, both to God and to his fellow-man, as is fully proved by the failures to do so by the wisest and best of the ancients. 2d. In such as he does discover and acknowledge, man frequently errs as to the mode in which they are to be discharged, as, for instance, when he feels, as has often been the case, his obligations to God, but thinks he may discharge them by offering human sacrifices. 3d. When both his duty and the manner of discharging them are known, conscience is yet often too obtuse or too weak, as we all know, to make men *feel* them, and impel men to a discharge of them. We therefore need additional means of securing both the knowledge and the enforcement of our duties to those which conscience, imperfect as we thus see that it is, can give.

5. In nature, God's revelation of himself is imperfect, and therefore our knowledge of what is due him, as well as of his will toward us, is imperfect. Nature does indeed reveal his existence, his power and wisdom, and his established principle of order, but it reveals: (1) Imperfectly his disposition of benevolence. (2) And nothing whatever of his character of holiness, except indeed it may be very imperfectly reflected from the moral character of his creature, man. (3) And if we should arrive at a conception of his holiness, there is yet no power revealed in nature by which sin may be overcome within us. Therefore, both from the imperfection of the knowledge given by nature, and from its total lack of moral power to aid us in carrying that knowledge into action, nature is insufficient, and a farther revelation is needed from God, manifesting his moral and spiritual nature in its perfection, and possessed of power over the human heart to frame it for right action. "In fine," we may well conclude with Paley, "I deem it unnecessary to prove that mankind stood in need of a revelation, because I have met with no serious person who thinks that even under the Christian revelation we have too much light."

From the very nature of the case, then, we perceive the total inadequacy of nature alone to suffice for the moral necessities of man, and we conclude the probability of a farther and direct revelation for *their* supply, at the hands of that wise and benevolent Creator and Preserver, who, in nature, has so bounteously and variously provided for his physical need and joy. This conclusion, we have seen, is confirmed by the general opinion of men, that such a revelation was necessary, as also by the greatest thinkers that have lived. It is farther exhibited in the utter confusion as to the most important doctrines that has always prevailed in the absence of such a revelation. And lastly, we have seen how much it is demanded by the dark view of the moral state of the whole world, in all times, without revelation. We claim, then, from this survey, that any *just a priori* improbability that Hume's objection may be thought to bring against revelation, because of the uniformity of the laws of nature and the improbability of miracle, is more than counterbalanced by this other, strong, opposing *a priori* improbability that this imperative need of man should never be supplied by the great and good God. While we concede such a general uniformity of nature, yet, remembering that God has not put it out of his own power to interfere with nature, and directly control her, and remembering too that science itself teaches us that several times, on extraordinary occasions—in creation, in the production of life, and in the bringing forth of man — he has so interfered for beneficent purposes, we must conclude that, for such high ends as we have pointed out, he would once more so interfere in our behalf, and work even miracles to give us a revelation of himself, of our destiny, and of his will.

6. Hume's objection is thus fallacious in the incorrectness of its statement of the facts. It is fallacious too in not recognizing the antecedent probability of a revelation as opposing the *a priori* improbability of a miracle. It is, thirdly, fallacious in its argument itself, in that it really begs the question in dispute. For, by saying that "the proof against a miracle is as entire as any argument from experience can be," etc., he can surely mean nothing less than that a miracle is something wholly unknown to all human experience, and that the laws of nature have been always uniform. This is the whole point of his argument. But this is the very point in dispute. We claim that, even as it is recorded in the Bible, many thousands, in different countries and ages, and sometimes through a long series of years—from the

passage of the Red Sea by the Israelites, and their daily supply of manna for forty years in the wilderness, to the feeding of the thousands by Christ, and afterward—miracles were openly witnessed by multitudes of people. If the Bible account is doubted, or alleged to be false, that is another and a *prior* question, which must be settled by showing, *on other grounds*, that the evidence for their truth is insufficient, contradictory, or disproved by other evidence. But we cannot say the Bible is false, simply because it tells of the occurrence of miracles, and miracles are impossible, and then argue that miracles are impossible, because we are nowhere credibly told of their occurrence. The latter is the argument of Hume, given without any previous impeachment on extraneous grounds of the credibility of the Scripture narrative. His position, then, that miracles are unknown to human experience, really begs the very point at issue—a point which, like all *questions of fact*, can only be finally settled by a full and impartial consideration of the testimony for or against, not by abstract reasoning of what is and what is not antecedently probable.

7. Finally, it may be safely claimed, in opposition to the position taken in the objection, that there is no miracle so great but that hu-

man testimony may establish it. Our minds are so formed that their assent is absolutely compelled to be given whenever a certain amount and kind of evidence have been given. "The evidence," as Campbell says, "arising from human testimony, in point of fact, is not altogether derived from experience, but, on the contrary, our doubt about testimony arises from experience. In reality, the constitution of our nature *obliges* us to believe the testimony of thousands of our fellow-men—and these, too, men of strict integrity, swayed by no motives of ambition or interest, and governed by the principles of common sense—of things to which they were themselves the actual witnesses." "If twelve men, in short," as Paley shows, "should testify to the same miraculous fact, and continue to repeat it, though at the risk of life, through many years, separate and apart, in opposition to many keen and watchful opponents, and before various tribunals of justice, and if their testimony should nevertheless perfectly agree, and be corroborated by all the other witnesses in the case, and by all the attendant circumstances discoverable, it may be truly said that the human mind could not resist such testimony."

Whether Christianity has such testimony to its truth, we will hereafter discuss. We now claim that it has been shown that miracles, and consequently a revelation, may be established by human testimony. The objection which denies it is shown to be without force—nay, a strong antecedent probability is seen to exist in its favor; and we therefore bring this stage of our inquiry to a close with the affirmation of the Competency of Evidence in general to prove Miracles, and therefore to establish the fact of a revelation given of God.

CHAPTER IV.

THE COMPETENCY OF THE EVIDENCE—II. PROBABLE EVIDENCE IS SUFFICIENT TO PROVE A REVELATION.

THE next possible objection to the Christian Evidences is that they consist only of probable, and not demonstrative, evidence, and are therefore insufficient. This objection asserts that, inasmuch as the best human testimony is liable to error, revelation is not proved thereby, beyond the possibility of a doubt, and consequently the evidence is inadequate. This brings us to consider the Competency of the Evidence in its second point—namely, the Sufficiency of Probable Evidence to Prove a Revelation.

It is sufficient, because it is unreasonable and absurd to require any greater than probable evidence of the facts of the Christian religion. Whately has remarked, in his Annotations on Bacon's Essays, that the "craving for infallibility in religious matters is a fruitful cause of atheism. Some, because they think that revelation is not such as it is reasonable and proper for God to bestow, choose to reject it, thus claiming for themselves infallibility of judgment as to what is reasonable and proper, and judging God; others, because they think some system of theology—some particular interpretation of the Bible—to be wrong, reject the Bible itself with the theological system—as if the possession of a divine revelation insured the presence also of an infallible interpreter." In like manner others, as unreasonably and absurdly, reject Christianity because its evidences are probable only, and not demonstrative—that is, that it establishes its facts only beyond a reasonable doubt, but not beyond all possibility of objection by their own minds. In opposition to such a notion, we assert that probable evidence is alone applicable to the case in hand. Demonstrative evidence is totally inapplicable to the establishment not only of the facts of Christianity, but to that of any facts whatever.

1. Demonstrative evidence consists solely in that evidence which arises from our reasoning from primary axioms of abstract *principles* to other abstract truths. Wholly abstract, therefore, and disconnected with any matter of fact, it is limited in its application entirely to the relations of number and quantity, and capable of establishing mathematical truth alone. "The field of demonstration," says Reid ("Intellect-

ual Powers of Man"), "is necessary truth; the field of probable reasoning is contingent truth —*i. e.*, not what *necessarily* must be at all times, but what is, or was, or shall be. . . . The strength of probable reasoning, for the most part, depends not upon any one argument, but upon many which unite their force, and lead to the same conclusion. Any one of them by itself would be insufficient to convince, but the whole taken together may have a force that is irresistible; so that to desire more evidence would be absurd. Would any man seek new arguments to prove that there were such persons as King Charles I. and Oliver Cromwell? Such evidence may be compared to a rope made up of many slender filaments twisted together. The rope has strength more than sufficient to bear the stress laid upon it, though no one of the filaments of which it is composed would be sufficient for it." Such are the principles of evidence laid down by Reid the philosopher, in his great work on the human mind, as the rules that must govern in all our decisions. In addition, we must remember that at its best the human mind is not infallible, and therefore all its knowledge whatsoever is liable to error—that none of its conclusions are ever really put beyond the possibility of a doubt. The very fact that evidence is necessary to us in order to establish a truth shows that we are beings of limited powers. (*Vide* Essay, by the Hon. W. E. Gladstone, *Fortnightly Review*, May, 1879, on "Probability as the Guide of Conduct."). If we were not, we should be able to recognize whatever is true immediately, without the aid of intermediate evidence; but if our powers are limited, they are always liable to make mistake. Not that they will necessarily err. A being of the most limited powers, while always liable to error, may yet always hit the truth; and therefore it is that we are still capable of attaining to a real knowledge of the truth, though we are fallible, and therefore that probable evidence may form a valid ground for confidence in our conclusions. But still there remains the fact that all our mental faculties are in themselves imperfect; their operations also, and their acts, are never infallible, and therefore their conclusions are always open to some degree of doubt. The demand, then, that Christian Evidences should be free from all doubt is unreasonable and absurd.

2. But not only are such the conclusions of abstract reasoning, but these are the principles that are practically and constantly followed in trials by our judicial tribunals. Greenleaf, the standard legal authority on the subject, in his

work "On Evidence," in his chapter, in vol. 1, on the "Nature and Principles of Evidence" (Italics ours), says: "None but mathematical truth is *susceptible* of that high degree of evidence called demonstration which excludes all possibility of error. *Matters of fact are proved by moral evidence* ALONE; by which is meant not only that kind of evidence which is employed on subjects connected with moral conduct, but all the evidence which is not obtained either from intuition or demonstration. In the ordinary affairs of life we do not require demonstrative evidence, because it is inconsistent with the nature of the subject, and to insist upon it would be to be unreasonable and absurd. The most that can be affirmed of such things is that there is no reasonable doubt concerning them. *The true question, therefore, in trials of fact is not whether it is possible that the testimony may be false, but whether there is a sufficient probability of its truth*—that is, whether the facts are shown by competent and satisfactory evidence. Things established by competent and satisfactory evidence are said to be proved. . . . It is assumed (*i. e.*, by objectors to this position) that all that men know is due to perception and reflection. But the knowledge acquired by an individual through his own perception and reflection is but a small part of what he possesses, much of what we are content to regard and act upon as knowledge having been acquired through others. Indeed, if man is to believe only upon his own personal experience, the world can neither be governed nor improved, and society must remain in the state in which it was left by the first generation of men. The disposition to believe may be termed instinctive. It is true that, in receiving the testimony of others, we are much influenced by its accordance with facts previously known or believed, and this constitutes what is termed its probability. Statements thus probable are received upon evidence much less cogent than we require for the belief of those which do not accord with our previous knowledge. Nevertheless, we should beware of distrusting all others. While unbounded credulity is the attribute of weak minds, unlimited skepticism belongs only to those who make their own knowledge and observation the exclusive standard of probability. Thus the King of Siam rejected the testimony of the Dutch embassador, that in his country water was sometimes congealed into a solid mass. Skeptics, inconsistently enough with their own principles, yet true to the nature of man, continue to receive a large portion of their knowledge upon testimony not derived from their own experience, but from that of other men, even when it is at variance with much of their own personal observation. Thus the testimony of the historian is received with confidence in regard to the occurrences of ancient times; that of the naturalist and traveler, in regard to the natural history and civil condition of other countries; that of the astronomer, respecting the heavenly bodies — facts which, upon the narrow basis of his own 'firm and unalterable experience,' upon which Mr. Hume so much relies, he would be bound to reject as wholly unworthy of belief."

Such are the principles constantly followed, in decisions made as to matters of fact, in our courts of justice. They are reasonably to be taken as rules which, having been settled by the wisest jurists, through centuries of discussion, are proper to guide us in the formation of our opinion as to questions of fact. Demonstrative evidence is by them utterly excluded. Demonstrative evidence, then, cannot be reasonably demanded of the truth of the facts of the Christian religion. Christianity asks nothing more than that her claims be subjected to the ordinary tests established for the ascertainment of facts. Those who require that they shall be proved by demonstrative evidence are unreasonable in the highest extreme, and their demand is wholly absurd.

3. Farther still, science also, in whose name the demand for demonstrative evidence is sometimes brought, follows the same principles; for the truth of the laws of nature also is dependent on human testimony. The facts from which those laws are deduced—*e. g.*, the observations of astronomy, botany, physics, etc.—for much the greater part can be furnished by others only, and not perceived individually by that one (*e. g.*, Newton) who deduces from them those laws.

Moreover, since no fact whatever can be proved to exist by demonstrative evidence as is a mathematical problem, the facts upon which science herself, infallible as she is supposed to be, builds her deductions, are also liable to be mistaken; for whether obtained through the use of the microscope, or of chemical experiment, etc., they are obtained only by observation and experiment, and therefore are all established by no more than probable evidence, and liable to be erroneous, and to lead to erroneous conclusions. The constant conflict in the testimony of the most scientific experts, given in judicial cases, proves this. After having had the best opportunities of examination, and using the best instruments and chemicals, and with their professional reputation at stake, the leading representatives of their several professions will yet *usually* come into court, after examining the same spot of blood, or the same body, and, instead of testifying alike, two or three will swear positively that the blood in question is human blood, or the body contains poison, while as many others will swear as positively directly to the contrary.*

Accordingly Jevous, an acknowledged authority on the subject ("Principles of Science," vol. i., pp. 244, 271, *et seq.*), lays down the following: "I conceive that it is impossible even to expound the principles and motives of induction, as applied to natural phenomena, in a sound manner, without resting them upon the theory of probability. Perfect knowledge alone can give certainty, and in nature perfect

---

* Thus in a case cited in 4 *American Law Journal*, 625, on a question of forgery of a signature, among other conflicts of testimony between men of the highest scientific authority, in examining whether "under the ink of the disputed signature the microscope brought to light marks of tracing," Dr. Charles T. Jackson, a "specialist in this line of extraordinary skill and reputation, and Prof. Horsford, well known for his accomplishments in the same line, backed by other experts of distinction," swore positively that it did, and Profs. Agassiz and Oliver Wendell Holmes that it did not.

knowledge would be infinite knowledge, which is clearly beyond our capacities. We have therefore to content ourselves with partial knowledge — knowledge mingled with ignorance, and producing doubt. . . . We can never recur too often to the truth, that our knowledge of the laws and future events of the external world is only probable. . . . Whatever feeling is actually present to the mind is certainly known to that mind. If I see blue sky, I may be quite sure that I do experience the sensation of blueness. . . . In the second place, we may have certainty of inference. The first axioms of Euclid are certainly true, . . . and whatever truth there is in the premises I can certainly embody in their direct logical result. . . . But I never can be quite sure that two colors are exactly alike, that two magnitudes are exactly equal, or that two bodies, whatsoever, are identical, even in their apparent relations. . . . Inferences which we draw concerning natural objects are never certain, except in a hypothetical point of view."

Science too, then, must rest her whole system upon the very same kind of evidence as supports revelation; and Christianity, to judge whose claims she has by some of her followers been arrogantly claimed to be the supreme arbiter, is bound to confront her, on her own ground, with equal support of truth. Probable evidence is, and can be, the only ground of confidence in each, as it is, and alone can be, of all our knowledge derived from matters of fact.

4. The speculative reasoning then of philosophers, the practical administration of justice in the courts, and the deductive reasonings of science, thus unite in acknowledging probable evidence sufficient to decide matters of fact. We adduce, finally, the course of daily, ordinary life, as showing by the constant conduct of men their real opinion of its sufficiency to decide our actions in matters pertaining to this life, and we claim therefore that it should also decide in the same way our action in respect to religion. "Probable evidence, in its very nature, affords but an imperfect kind of information, but to us is the very guide of life, . . . but being often repeated, will amount even to moral certainty—as, *e. g.*, the ebb and flow of the tide. . . . It is thought by some that if the evidence of revelation appears doubtful, this itself turns into a positive argument against it; . . . [whereas], in questions of difficulty, if there appears, on the whole, a greater presumption on one side than on the other, *this* determines the question, and lays us

under an *absolute* obligation to act upon that presumption. Nay, in questions of great consequence, a reasonable man will act upon presumptions such as amount to no more than to show that one side is as credible as another, as in numberless cases in the common pursuits of life, where a man would be thought, in a literal sense, distracted, who would not act, and with great application too, not only upon an even chance, but upon much less (*e. g.*, where health, fortune, or life, are at stake). . . . Besides, the evidence of religion not *appearing* obvious (*i. e.*, the fact that the evidence of religion may not seem entirely sufficient to them at first sight), may be part of some men's trial, and give scope for a virtuous exercise or vicious neglect of the understanding in examining or not examining into it. The man who had a right *disposition*, such as would lead him to follow the *precepts* of religion, if proved to be true, would be led, were he unconvinced, seriously to *consider* its *evidence*. Negligence before conviction is as really guilty as disobedience afterward. And even doubtful evidence puts men in a state of probation. . . . If a man were in *doubt* whether his entire temporal blessings did not come from a certain person, he could not consider himself in the same situation with regard to such person as if he had no [such] doubt; but there would be required from him reverence, careful consideration, openness to farther light and conviction. Doubt as much implies *some* evidence as belief a *higher* degree of it, and certainty a higher degree still. For, when we say there is an even chance, there is more evidence for *either* side of the question than there is for the truth of some idea that has come at random into the mind. But a disregard of even the lower degrees of evidence in our practice proves unfairness, and, in religion, corruptness of heart."— *Butler's Analogy.*

That probability is thus necessarily the very guide of life is not a conclusion held by Christians only, nor has it been used only to establish the claims of religion. Voltaire, in an essay upon judicial inquiries, says: "Almost all of human life turns upon probabilities. All that is not demonstrated to the eyes, or recognized as true by those clearly interested to deny, is at most only probable. . . . Uncertainty being almost always the lot of man, you will determine very seldom, if you expect a demonstration. In the meantime an opinion must be formed, and it should not be formed at random. It is then necessary to our feeble nature, blind, always subject to error, to study the probabilities with as much care as we learn arithmetic and geometry."*

Christianity, therefore, in possessing probable evidence, has, so far as its kind is concerned, all the evidence that we do or can require in our decisions in all—the most ordinary as well as the gravest—affairs of life. It has all that is possible to be applied to the ascertainment of matters of fact, all that is ever resorted to in such ascertainment in courts of law, and all that natural science can ever pretend to have in her acquirements of *data* necessary to her deductive conclusions. That evidence, then, is competent to establish her claims, and it is unreasonable and absurd to demand demonstrative evidence, or evidence concerning which there can be imagined no possible doubt. The denial of the competency of probable evidence, in matters of fact, to

---

* The original is as follows: "Presque toute le vie humane roule sur des probabilités. Tout ce qui n'est pas démontré aux yeux, ou reconnu pour vrai par les parties évidemment intérressées à le nier n'est tout au plus que probable. . . . L'incertitude étant presque toujours le partage de l'homme, vous détermineriez trés-rarement, si vous attendiez une démonstration. Cependant il faut prendre un parti; et il ne faut pas le prendre au hasard. Il est donc nécessaire à notre nature faible, aveugle, toujours sujette à l'erreur, d'étudier les probabilités avec autant de soin, que nous apprenous l'arithmétique et la géométrie."

command our belief, and consequently secure our obedience, must logically lead to the denial of the establishment of every fact, and render human knowledge impossible. Accordingly, to such a conclusion does Hume, the great objector to the testimony offered by Christianity, come. He concludes ("Treatise of Human Nature," Book I., Part 4, Sec. 1)—first, that all that is called human knowledge is only probability; and, secondly, that this probability, when duly examined, evanishes by degrees, and leaves at last no evidence at all; so that in the issue there is no ground to believe any one proposition rather than its contrary, and "all those are certainly fools who reason, or believe any thing." To such an extremity of universal skepticism must the denial of the competency of probable evidence logically lead, and actually often does lead, in more cases than Hume's. But surely such a conclusion as this is not the highest result of human reason, or the best for human interests. "He who makes wisdom," says Augustin (as quoted by Van Oosterzee), "consist in abstinence from all assent, makes it merely the confession of ignorance, and identifies it with nullity." Our reason cannot agree with this. We must believe that knowledge is attainable by man, and therefore that to the attainment of that knowledge evidence that is probable is sufficient.

Concluding, then, that the evidence, in all its aspects, is in its nature wholly competent, we still have to show, in order to establish its entire admissibility, and, so far as the truth of the facts is concerned, its worthiness for our acceptance—leaving their weight to be afterward estimated—that the record of those facts, as contained in the New Testament Scriptures, is a true account, and is neither forged nor falsified. This topic comprises what is called the Authenticity of the Evidence, and will form the subject of the following chapter.

CHAPTER V.

THE AUTHENTICITY OF THE EVIDENCE.

The next question that claims our attention is that of the trustworthiness, or authenticity, of the evidence offered. This relates merely to the truth of the Gospel history, and, without considering their weight, examines only whether the occurrences related in that history, and on which Christianity is founded, are truly related, and actually took place. This will form the last question in our consideration of the Admissibility of the Evidence; and, if its examination concludes in favor of the truth of that record—the competency of evidence in general being already established—we must admit that the evidence that therein is actually offered is in itself genuine and trustworthy, and of a nature proper to be used for the establishment of Christianity. The weight to which that evidence is entitled, in proving the divinity of Christianity, is a farther question, and one that will next engage our attention.

To show that that history is true, we cite exactly the same kind of proofs, but in a much higher degree, as in establishing the authenticity of any other ancient writings, and such as are universally admitted in all other cases to be sufficient to establish authenticity beyond all reasonable doubt. These are the concurrent testimony of contemporaneous and succeeding authors; the difficulty of a forgery, in the very nature of the case; the internal marks of authenticity, in the language of the book, its style, and its agreement within itself; its agreement with the customs, manners, and history, of the time and country in which it professes to have been written; the character of its author or authors for truth and accuracy of information; the merit of the work itself, in moral character, worth, and dignity; the fact of great changes having taken place in the world's history through the facts they allege to have occurred; the present existence of world-wide and powerful institutions—as, *e. g.*, the Christian Church—alleged to have derived their origin from those facts, and of whose origin—greatest of earthly institutions, as they are, and having their beginning, without doubt, in an age and a country highly enlightened, and of whose history we have a minute account—we have no other explanation, nor even any probable hypothesis. These, and such like proofs, are held sufficient fully to decide the truth of any alleged facts of past times.

Very seldom, if indeed in any single case, do they all coincide to establish the truth of any ancient writings whatever, except that of the Gospel history; and used separately, as they are continually, to test the authenticity of other ancient writings, and combining, as they do, to attest the validity of the Gospels, we must concede that its truth is proved beyond all reasonable doubt. To exhibit the force of that proof, we will present the evidence to show—first, that the Gospel account existed at, or at least immediately after, the time and in the place when and where its alleged facts occurred; and, secondly, that thus existing, as it did, where detection was easy and certain, it could never have gained acceptance or escaped an exposure, if it had been an imposture, and its alleged facts had never happened.

1. The Gospel histories were written in the countries, and very soon after the time, in which the events they record took place.

(1) We have the external testimony of other authors living near the same time and place to this fact. "We receive," writes Horne (Introduction, etc.), from whom much of the following argument is drawn, "the works of Matthew, Mark, etc., for the same reasons that we receive those of Xenophon, Cæsar, etc., . . . but in a much stronger degree. For, very dif-

ferently from the classics, the New Testament was read over three-quarters of the world, while other authors were limited to one nation, or country—were read publicly and often, and were acknowledged by large societies to be the writings of apostles and others, as they profess. An uninterrupted succession of writers, from the apostolic times down—some friends, some enemies—either quote from or make allusions to them. Translations were made in the second century, which were greatly multiplied in the course of one or two centuries, so that forgery became absolutely impossible, unless we suppose that men of different nations, sentiments, languages, and often exceedingly hostile to each other, should all agree in one forgery. But if we are to do this, we may throw aside all the writings in the world, and reject human testimony altogether." But it is evident that, if not genuine, the Gospels must be forgeries, and forgeries too of later ages, since a forged history could certainly not be palmed off upon the age itself of which it gave its false history. Yet it is equally evident that a forgery in such later age, when it would have had to have been published at once in various and widely-separated languages and countries, and, more still, as the sacred writings which had been held by them and their fathers, through several generations, to comprise the supreme rule of their conduct—it is evident that such an imposition as this would have been impossible.

Moreover, all the marks of forgery are wanting. To give us a reasonable ground for suspicion, even, that a work is spurious, there must exist at least one of the following circumstances: (1) Doubts entertained from its appearance in the world as to its genuineness; or (2), denials by immediate friends of the pretended author, who were able to decide upon the subject; or (3), a long series of years elapsed after his death, in which the book was unknown; or (4), a style different from his other writings, or different from what might reasonably be expected; or (5), events recorded that happened later than the time of the pretended author; or (6), opinions recorded contrary to those he was known to hold. But not one of these can be pretended to hold against the genuineness of the Gospel histories. It is unreasonable and unjust, then, to charge them with being forgeries of a later date, merely from self-will, and without any ground of rejection.

On the other hand, we have a succession of writers, friendly and hostile, quoting and alluding to the things recorded in the Gospels, as well-known facts, running up to the apostolic age. In the fourth century we have numerous writers, such as Jerome, Eusebius, Augustin, Athanasius, etc. Ten catalogues are given, of which six name the books we now have, and no others; and, of the other four, three omit Revelation only, and one, by Philaster, of Brescia, omits Hebrews and Revelation only—both which he, however, expressly acknowledges in his other works. In the third century, Origen, Gregory, Cyprian, and other Christians, various heretical sects, and the Emperor Julian the Apostate (an infidel), all bear their testimony. In the second century we have Tertullian, of Carthage, first an orthodox, afterward an heretical, writer; Clement, of Alexandria; Theophilus, of Antioch; Athenagoras, of Athens; Irenæus, of Lyons; Melito, of Sardis; Hegesippus, a converted Jew; Tatian, Justin Martyr, of Palestine; and Papias, of Hieropolis—all of whom mention some of the books, and some nearly all the books, of the New Testament. And besides these, Marcion, the Sabellians, Arians, Donatists, Novatians, Manicheans, and other heretics, with Celsus and Porphyry, infidels and bitter enemies of Christianity, all make various allusions to the New Testament books, and without intimating a doubt of their authenticity. And in the first century, at widely-separated distances, the following widely-differing writers do the same, viz.: Barnabas and Clement, the fellow-laborers of Paul; Hermas, their contemporary (*vide* Rom. xvi. 14); Ignatius, who was Bishop of Antioch, A.D. 70; Polycarp, of Smyrna, a disciple of St. John, and who died about A.D. 166; Cerinthus, a heretic, contemporary with St. John, and the Ebionites.

At greater detail Row (Bampton Lectures, 1877) shows the weight of this testimony, as follows: 1. Irenæus, Clement, and Tertullian, toward the end of the second century, as clearly recognized the Gospels as of canonical authority as we. 2. Marcion's Gospel, A.D. 140, was a mutilated copy of Luke's. 3. The Gospels used by the authors above are of very corrupt text, and therefore must have been in existence some time. 4. Papias, who died about A.D. 163, mentions Matthew and Luke. 5. The Apostolic Fathers mention them. Justin Martyr, who wrote A.D. 145–150, and whose life therefore brings us back to within eighty or eighty-five years of the death of Christ, or about as long as that of Wesley to our own times, speaks of the Memoirs of the Apostles, and "the Gospels," which were publicly read in the Church. 6. Clement, of Rome, Polycarp, and Ignatius, whose lives covered even earlier periods, also refer to the same facts as are contained in the Gospels. Now, the references in Justin are about two hundred in number, one hundred and ninety-six of which, for all practical purposes, are the same as those recorded in the Gospels. It is certain too that he used some *documents* which he designates as "Gospels." Now, if these were different from those we have—*i. e.*, as to their authorship—then we have merely additional accounts of our Lord's life and words, and their historical reality is so much the more assured; and the more numerous the documents, the more is it assured, since the greater the number of witnesses testifying to the same facts, the more conclusively are those facts proved. The same is true also of the earlier Fathers, and proves that the traditions embodied in the Gospels must have been accepted by the Church in a written or oral form during the last twenty years of the first century, and, also, if there were then traditions of a different form current, they were afterward rejected. But Christ was crucified about the thirty-third year of the first century; there was then an interval of certainly no more than forty-seven to sixty-seven years between his death and the first existence of those accounts. In so short a time it would not have been possible to forge such legends, and impose them upon a considerable body of men, scattered over so wide an expanse of country as were the Christian Churches, and that in the face of the great opposition both of the Jews and the heathen.

These considerations justly entitle us to claim that the Gospels, as we have them, existed very soon after Christ's crucifixion. We observe farther:

2. The narrative bears indisputable evidence internally that it is genuine. 1st. The confidence with which the authors narrate their story shows them to be writers addressing their contemporaries on matters well known to each. 2d. Their numerous and minute allusions to the manners and customs of the time and nation, and to the geography of the country, in which they profess to have lived, prove their genuineness. Their familiar acquaintance with the religious ceremonies of the Jews, the prevalence, in their writings, of words, phrases, and thoughts, derived from the Old Testament, prove that they were Jews; and so as to their continual references to the ordinary habits of the people, and to the physical characteristics of the country of Palestine.*

---

*Van Lennep, the acknowledged authority on the subject, says ("Bible Lands," p. 807): "These facts furnish an overwhelming argument for the authenticity of the

3d. The language and style in which they are written prove the same thing beyond controversy. Greek was at that time a sort of universal language as English is now. Of course, when used by a nation not Greek, it almost certainly became intermixed with many

Scriptures. Not only their topography but the manners and customs of the people therein depicted give evidence on every page that the Bible was written in Western Asia, and by Asiatics, about the time claimed. It could have been penned nowhere else, and by no other people. So many minute and, in themselves considered, insignificant circumstances are woven into the narrative as to make deceit or imposture an utter impossibility. Let an Occidental take up any Bible narrative, and attempt to reproduce it in his own words with an equal degree of minuteness, and before many minutes an Oriental audience would be sure to show unmistakable signs of mirth, on account of the incongruity of some of his details. If he does not, like the colored preacher, speak of Martha as 'busy frying fritters,' he cannot well avoid, in some other way, showing the difference which exists between the habits of the West and those of the East. . . . And when we consider the many mistakes as to facts contained in the most carefully-written histories and narratives, and notice, at the same time, the perfect freedom of the Bible from all such mistakes, though it is a voluminous and extremely varied compilation, and many of its writers illiterate men, we cannot avoid the conclusion that we have in the present case something beyond mere authenticity. We see most unmistakable evidence that the authors of the Bible were guided and controlled in their work by the special influence of that Spirit which alone can never err."

peculiarities and forms of expression derived from the language of that nation—just as happens when a foreigner endeavors to speak English. Now, the Greek of the New Testament is not pure Greek, such as a native would write, but it is intermixed with many peculiarities such as belonged *exclusively* to the languages called the East-Aramean (or Hebrew), and West-Aramean (or Syriac)—the languages that were spoken, *at that time*, by the *Jews in Palestine*. But the total overthrow of Jerusalem by the Romans in the year A.D. 70—less than forty years after the crucifixion of Christ—and the consequent great slaughter and dispersion of the Jews, made great changes of all kinds, and, among others, *changed the language* greatly, so that in the succeeding generation, or sixty or seventy years after Christ, it would have been almost impossible to write in such a dialect. Besides, there was no one then who would have done so. The Jews would not certainly, and the only sects remaining in Palestine in the second century were Nazarenes and Ebionites, and they used but one Gospel, and that a translation in Hebrew. They would scarcely have forged a whole New Testament, and that too in Greek. The only reasonable conclusion is that the New Testament was written in the first century, and by natives of

Syria, as they profess. And the same conclusion is borne out by the character of the style in which its books are written. Plain and unadorned, the style of the Gospels shows that their authors were such as they are described—plain, unlearned men. In the Epistles of Paul, on the other hand, the learning displayed, the strong but irregular argument—the learning being that which only an educated Jew would likely possess, the whole style of argumentation that which a Jewish convert confuting his brethren on ground familiar to both would employ—both give good evidence that he is really the author. And so in general, the characteristics of both language and thought are those belonging to the persons, the time, and the occasions, from which they claim to have derived their origin.

4th. The very numerous circumstances related in the New Testament, and their agreement with the history of the times, prove its authenticity. Whoever undertakes to forge a set of writings, and ascribe them to persons who lived in another age, exposes himself to the utmost danger of a discrepancy with the history and manners of that age. Of all books there would be none so liable to detection as the New Testament, were it a forgery. The scene of action is not confined to a single city, but extends to the greatest cities of the Roman empire; and continual allusions are made to the various customs and opinions of the Greeks, the Romans, and the Jews. If then the New Testament, after the severest scrutiny, is found to harmonize perfectly with the history, the customs, and even the opinions, of the first century, and if the more minutely we inquire the more perfect we find the coincidence, we must conclude that it was beyond the power of human ability to forge it. Yet such is the fact. Space cannot here be given to even mention those numerous coincidences. The following, however, may be taken as examples of them, the whole number of which it has taken volumes to set forth (*vide* "Paley's Evidences," and his "Horæ Paulinæ," and "Blunt's Undesigned Coincidences"), viz.: The division of Palestine into the three principal provinces of Judea, Samaria, and Galilee; the existence of two chief religious sects, the Pharisees and Sadducees, among the Jews *of that period;* the standing of the temple still in Jerusalem, its visitation by Jews from all parts of the world, etc. Many of these are presupposed rather than formally stated—just as a genuine account would do—and there are more convincingly still many more minute and latent coincidences, abounding in the twenty-seven different books of the New Testament, which only a close and laborious study brings to light. (*Vide* Paley and Blunt, as above.) No forgery could so perfectly accomplish its work as this; and when we reflect, in addition, that those twenty-seven books were written, as their style undeniably shows, by several authors, the difficulty of forgery — simultaneously by several hands — is immensely increased. Add to this the fact that the most adverse criticism, after the longest and most searching seeking, has never yet succeeded in exposing *a single discrepancy* in the multitude of their incidental allusions and minute references to the history, customs, manners, and opinions, of Greeks, Romans, and Jews, and we must say that a forgery was wholly impossible. But if the Gospels are not forgeries, they are genuine, and were written at the time and place in which they profess to have been written.

From the latter consideration alone we might well come to this conclusion; but when we consider with it also the force of all the other various and independent preceding evidences which we have cited in support of the same conclusion, it is not only shown to be probably true, but morally certain. The confidence and familiarity with the circumstances apparent in the authors, the tongue in which they write—impossible to later writers—and the minute and perfect coincidence of their accounts with the manners, etc., of the times and countries, would alone be sufficient to prove the genuineness of the New Testament Scriptures; but when we add to all this their mention, and even quotation, and that without a single denial from any quarter, whether Christian, heretic, Jew, or infidel, by writers both friendly and hostile, extending to within fifty to seventy years, at the least, of Christ, we must conclude that the New Testament was in existence in the countries and at the time that is claimed for it.

2. It is still necessary, however, to show that the New Testament is a true account of the things it relates. Thus far we have shown only that it must have existed very soon after the crucifixion of Christ. But this does not make it at once obvious that it is therefore true. To prove that it is true will therefore be our next task, and will occupy the remainder of the chapter. We argue this from—

(1) The character of its authors. While the character of a witness is good and unimpeached, the presumption is that his testimony is true. It cannot be doubted that the authors of the New Testament were in a situation to know

concerning the facts they relate. They were the chief witnesses of some, and principal actors in others, of those facts. Their opportunities for correct information were therefore the best possible; and that they were also honest and truthful narrators, we also maintain. For (*vide* Row, Bampton Lectures, 1877), 1st. Their moral character, though rigidly tested then, and closely examined since, has never been impeached by any one, even by their bitterest opponents; 2d. The plainness and simplicity of their accounts show them to have been plain, simple men, *unable*, if they wished, to frame so vast, so highly ingenious, and so unrivaled, a scheme of fraud as this is, if it is an invented story; 3d. They had no interests to serve in doing so, for the New Testament was not calculated in any way to advance their worldly interests, but enjoins nothing but the utmost unworldliness and self-sacrifice on all its followers, and the promulgation of its principles actually brought upon them, throughout their lives, the most extreme miseries.

(2) The character of their accounts themselves. 1st. Their whole style of writing about the most astonishing events—*e. g.*, the raising of the dead, etc.—is so calm and argumentative—almost without a trace of emotion—as shows them to be any thing but enthusiasts,

and proves them therefore likely neither to be self-deceived nor desirous of deceiving others. 2d. Their plainness and simplicity in relating their own errors and faults—*e. g.*, in their forsaking and denial of Jesus in his hour of greatest need, as well as in telling unreservedly the lowliness of the birth and condition of their Lord, his rejection by his nation, his ignominious execution on the cross as a malefactor, etc. —this simple truth and frankness apparent gives good reason to conclude the truth of the whole. 3d. Their entire, substantial agreement proves its truth. They evidently write without any reference to each other. Their different arrangements of the matters they relate in common, their relation each of some facts which the others omit, and their relation of the same facts, varying as *truthful* witnesses looking from diverse stand-points always vary, but forgers never, prove this. Nevertheless, they all substantially agree—notably, *e. g.*, in the traits of character given of Jesus, and in the exhibition of his words and actions—the great foundation of Christianity. 4th. *They appeal themselves to proofs notorious at the time.* (*Vide* 1 Cor. i. 4, 5; ii. 4, 5; v. 3–5; xii.; xiii. 8; xiv. 1–33; 2 Cor. xii. 7–11; Gal. iii. 5; 1 Thess. i. 5.)

(3) There was a general and undisputed be-

lief in the facts narrated in the Gospels immediately after the death of Christ. The two Epistles of Paul to the Corinthians, and those to the Romans and Galatians, are now almost universally admitted, by even the most skeptical scholars, to be genuine and authentic, and written within twenty-eight years from the crucifixion of Christ, as also the two to the Thessalonians, and those to the Philippians and to Philemon, written A.D. 55 to A.D. 62. Being letters, they are of a species of documents now everywhere acknowledged to be of the very highest authority, and being written to Churches in which, as their contents show, there were parties hostile to Paul (*vide* Corinthians, Galatians, etc.), by whom any erroneous statement would have been instantly exposed, we may feel sure that all his statements as to the facts and doctrines believed at that time are entirely true. Now, we find that these letters, principally by their incidental allusions, but also by their direct statements, assert as undoubted truths all the principal facts related in the Gospels. 1st. They show that even then, less than thirty years after his crucifixion, Christ was *generally* considered, both by Paul himself and the whole Church, to be superhuman and divine; for in those Epistles it is declared that He is the "Son of

God," "over all God blessed forever," our future Judge; that he was crucified; that he was the object of prayer — the "one Lord" — that he was "preached;" and that no "other Jesus" was to be preached, nor "another gospel." (*Vide* 1 Cor. i. 1–3, 23, 30, 31; iv. 1–5; viii.; 2 Cor. xi. 3–5; Gal. i. 6–9; Phil. i. 15–18; Rom. i. 1–4; ix. 3–5; xiv. 4–12.) So in the Apocalypse, which is also admitted to be genuine, He is made "the Prince of the kings of the earth," the "First and Last," the Living One, who "was dead and is alive forevermore," and is worshiped in heaven. 2d. Baptism and the Supper are mentioned by Paul as then existing, Gal. iii. 27; 1 Cor. xi. 23–25; the resurrection, 1 Cor. xv.; the Lord's teaching referred to, 1 Cor. vii. 10–12; ix. 13, 14; Christ is set forth as the great subject of teaching, 2 Cor. iv. 3–6; iii. 18; Phil. iii. 8–10; as also 2 Pet. i. 8; iii. 18; 1 Cor. 23, 24; Eph. iv. 20, 21; 1 Cor. x. 31–33; xi. 1; Rom. xv. 1–3, 5, 6; Eph. iv. 17–21; Heb. ii. 1–4. These and other such passages prove — (1) that the Church was then in possession of some accounts of Christ; (2) that these were substantially the same as in our Gospels; and (3), that Christ, within thirty years of his death, was the great Object of their adoration and imitation.

(4) They brought many others into a like

firm belief of the things which they related, who before had even been enemies.

(5) There have universally existed, ever since those alleged events, certain commemorative ordinances, or monuments, of great celebrity, the observance of which can no more be accounted for, unless the facts, on which they are said to have been founded, really happened, than the observance of the Fourth of July in the United States, or Guy Fawkes Day in England. Such are Christian Baptism, the Lord's Supper, and the change, after Christ's resurrection, of the observance of the seventh day as a day of rest to that of the first—all of which are evidences of Christ's life, death, and resurrection, as of the Christian Church generally.

(6) *All* the testimony *that we have* from profane authors attest the same facts. Tacitus says (Annals, 66) that the Christians "took their name from one Christ, who, during the reign of Tiberius, was sentenced under Pilate." Lucianus (De Morte Peregrini, c. 11, 12, 13) expressly mentions his crucifixion, and calls Jesus "the great man who was crucified in Palestine;" and again, "the crucified sophist (or wise man), who had been the author of a new religion." Suetonius mentions (in Claudio, cap. 25) the fact of "the Jews rebelling

in Rome, *on the instigation of Christ*"—a false charge, indeed, as alleged against Christ, but necessarily testifying to the existence of Christ and his supposed great influence over the Jews. And Pliny, A.D. 110 (Epist. Plin. x. 97), says "that the Christians were accustomed to sing hymns to Christ as to a God." Besides these Romans, Josephus, the *Jewish* historian, says "In those days lived Jesus, a wise man, for he perpetrated several extraordinary works, and made many Jews and heathen his followers. When Pilate had condemned him, on the accusation of our most prominent men, those who first loved him did not forsake him. And to this day the sect of Christians, called after his name, has not died out" (Ant. xviii. 3, 3; cf. 5. 2, xx. 9, 1; D. B. J. vi. 5, 4). In the Jewish Mischna also, and the Gemara (*vide Princeton Review*, July, 1878, p. 118), calumnies against him and his mother, there contained, prove at least that the accounts of his miraculous conception and immaculate birth were then generally known. And, besides all these, there are remains existing of Christian art, monuments, emblematical representations, etc., dating back to the time of the Antonines, A.D. 138–180, and found in Italy—a long distance, in those days, from Palestine, where Christianity first arose—which testify also to the same facts. And the excavations in Pompeii have, in our own day, brought to light such evidences on the walls that still stand of her ruined houses.*

But Pompeii was destroyed A.D. 79. These remains, then, show that Christianity, and consequently its doctrines and facts, were known that early in that distant land. Indeed, the indisputable fact that the first persecution against the Christians broke out under Nero, "in the tenth year of his reign" (*vide* Gibbon's "Decline and Fall," etc., ch. ix., sec. 3), proves, beyond all controversy, that the Christian Church was then in existence as far even as Rome, and therefore its doctrines, and the great facts of Christ's life, death, and resurrection, upon which those doctrines are founded, were even then well known there, and believed.

(7) Furthermore, the facts thus presented make it evident, from the very nature of the case, that a forged account would have been impossible. As we have seen, so early as A.D. 64 — only about thirty years after Christ —

---

* One of these is the remains of scoffing jests against the Christians, scribbled on the walls, as, for instance, the words, "(*i*)*gni gaudi* (*C*)*hristianæ*"—" Be glad for there being fire, O Christians"—intended to mock at those Christians who were condemned to be burnt at the stake (*vide* Row's Bampton Lectures).

Christianity had reached as far as Rome, and also had had time to make such progress there as to excite a persecution against them. But, as Row mentions, Sir G. C. Lewis, in his work on the "Credibility of Early Roman History," for the purposes of a critical examination into the authenticity of the early Roman traditions, has shown that if an account be published within even eighty or ninety years of the time in which the facts it professes to relate occurred, it is still within the period of genuine historical tradition, and capable of having its authenticity fully tested by the knowledge of those events, still current among the people. Thus, the battle of Waterloo, or even the American Revolution, which was one hundred years ago, may thus be tested. Many persons are living who have had the accounts of those times from their fathers, and some even of those who took part in them may remain. A popular knowledge of them thus exists throughout the countries which they have particularly affected. Now, it would be manifestly impossible to impose upon the people that such transactions had not then taken place. It would be equally impossible to persuade people within such a period that great transactions had then taken place of which they had never known personally, nor ever before heard. But when we try so to impose upon the world, only twenty or thirty years after the alleged facts are said to have occurred, and persuade people that great public events had then occurred, when they had never even been heard of, success is surely impossible. Yet this is what we must believe as to the history of the Gospels, if it is a forgery. Its accounts were circulated certainly as early as twenty to thirty years after the facts it relates are alleged to have taken place, and that too in the very country where they were said to have occurred. Those accounts state that those facts excited the greatest public commotions and tumults; they recite events of the most remarkable and miraculous character, said to have happened in the presence of multitudes; and they are put forth with an air of the greatest assurance that those facts were indisputable. Surely, if it had not been generally known that they had taken place, those accounts could never have obtained credence for a single hour. The inhabitants of Palestine would, on hearing them, begin to ask, How was it they had never before heard of this Jesus, who was said to have traveled, time and again, only twenty years ago, or less, over all the country, conspicuously presenting himself in all their most public places, preaching constantly in their synagogues to the assembled congregations; driving out the traders from the temple; followed by thousands about the country; *working miracles by scores*, so that he healed the sick, made the blind to see, the dumb to talk; and even raised the dead, and fed the thousands in the desert; at last was greeted by the multitudes at their own great Passover-feast at Jerusalem with hosannas as their Messiah; afterward apprehended, tried publicly, first by their own chief tribunal, and then before the Roman governor; then executed on the cross, with the accompaniment of a remarkable darkness over the land, an *earthquake*, and the *rending of the vail of the temple?* Surely, if they had never before heard of these things, they would have received such accounts with contempt, and rejected them at once with scorn.

That they did not do so, but, on the contrary, in great numbers received and believed them, to the loss often of property, liberty, and life, proves that those accounts were known to be true. If they had not been true, moreover, both the Jews—who from the first were most violent enemies of Christianity, and the Romans, who, as we have seen, soon became their most cruel persecutors, having together, as they had, all the power of the government, and all the means of investigation at their sole command—would have been able to detect and expose this imposture of the poor and despised Christians, who had no resources of wealth or power whatever. And they would certainly have done so, and shown and put on record, as they could have done, the falseness of those alleged public and notorious miracles, etc., of Jesus. That no one of them ever did it at any time during the three hundred years of the first period of Christianity, when it was persecuted throughout the Roman empire with the most dreadful cruelty and bloodshed, proves that such exposure was impossible, because there was no such imposture. That the Christian religion continued to grow through those three hundred years, till at last it became the mistress of the empire, proves that men knew then that its facts were true.

In addition to all this, let us again weigh such consideration as the following, already mentioned: Its authors had no worldly motive to serve by inventing such a false story. The fact that it was not the established religion of any nation for three hundred years, makes it perfectly absurd to suppose it the offspring of priestcraft or political contrivance. Indeed, in its very character, teaching as it does the utmost self-abnegation as the highest duty of man, it is *not* adapted to further any worldly interests; and in point of fact, its promulgation did subject them, through long years, to the severest sufferings. "If the apostles were all honest, they were incapable of such deception; if they were all knaves, they were unlikely to labor to make men virtuous; but if some were honest, and some cheats, the latter could not have so deceived the former as to matters of fact."—*Horne.* Nor would their accounts so wonderfully agree.

(8) Finally, the portraiture of Christ which we have in the Gospels could never, as Row shows us (Bampton Lectures, 1877), have been the creation of any human genius. As we shall see hereafter, some of the most eminent skeptics themselves unite in declaring that He is unquestionably the grandest Character in history. Mill, in the last of his posthumous essays, says: "It is of no use to say that Christ, as exhibited in the Gospels, is not historical. . . . Who among his disciples, or among their proselytes, was capable of inventing the sayings ascribed to Jesus, or of imagining the life and character revealed in the Gospels? Certainly not the fishermen of Galilee, certainly not St. Paul, and still less the early Christian writers, in whom nothing was more evident than that the good which was in them was all derived, as they all professed that it was, from

a higher source." And so Rousseau asserts that the inventor of such a story would be "a more wonderful character than the hero."

"It is a palpable fact that this great character, though made up in its delineation of a vast number of parts, or, in other words, of all the facts recorded in the Gospels, yet forms not a mere congeries of materials, but a perfect unity; and no theory can give a philosophical account of this fact except that the Gospels are, in all their main outlines, truly historical. That it was of deliberate invention, and that a character which, as Lecky (a skeptic) says, has proved to be 'the greatest incentive to holiness,' is itself the product of conscious fraud, is so intrinsically incredible that it has been abandoned even by all the great leaders of modern unbelief. Nor could it be the product of self-delusion, or the agglomeration of myths and legends accumulating in the course of time. Its unquestionable unity and perfection could never have so originated. Even as the creation of a single genius, it has been said by Rousseau to have been impossible; but we have here four delineations, each contributing, and all necessary, to the perfect whole. And if we suppose it the product of myths, then it was the creation not only of the persons who originally invented them, but of as many more as contributed to them, in whatever degree, and therefore of a large number. Now, these could never have so agreed unless the Personage they describe had been a reality; for never have men been able to invent a character at once exhibiting— (1) The most perfect manifestation of benevolence, tempered with holiness; (2) absolute unselfishness, the contrary never appearing in a single act or word; (3) the highest and most unique self-assertion, united with the most perfect humility; (4) the same ideal of morality, preserved throughout in all the Gospels; (5) in fine, perfect moral perfection, without one spot. The legendary spirit never invented any thing of a moral type so elevated as this; nor, if it could, would the several succeeding writers have likely concurred in selecting only the elevated myths, and neglecting all of a contrary character; nor, if they had, would such a chastened edition of the legends have so entirely gained acceptance with the popular mind; nor, finally, could so exquisite a picture of moral character ever have been formed by such a mode of selection and simple juxtaposition, any more than a beautiful picture by a painter selecting portions of other inferior works, and merely joining them together."

Now, to all the foregoing testimony apply

the accepted rules governing our assent to facts which are sought to be established by evidence. "In the second place [*i. e.*, next to the first general ground of evidence—viz., our natural confidence in testimony—as referred to in the preceding chapter], evidence," says Greenleaf ("Evidence," *id.* as above), "rests upon our general experience of the truth of the statements of men of integrity, having capacity and opportunity for observation, and without apparent influence from passion or interest to pervert the truth. This belief is strengthened by our previous knowledge of the narrator's reputation for veracity, by the absence of conflicting testimony, and by the presence of that which is corroborating and cumulative. Again, the third basis of evidence is the known and experienced connection subsisting between collateral facts or circumstances, satisfactorily proved, and the fact in controversy . . . connections either physical or moral. In the actual occurrences of human life nothing is inconsistent. Every event which actually transpires has its appropriate relation and place in the vast complications of circumstances, of which the affairs of men consist; it owes its origin to those which have preceded it; it is intimately connected with all others which occur at the same time and place, and often with those of remote regions, and in its turn gives birth to a thousand others which succeed. In all this there is a perfect harmony; so that it is hardly possible to invent a story which, if closely compared with all the actual contemporaneous occurrences, may not be shown to be false." Take these principles —which, with that of our natural belief in the testimony of others, constitute all the basis of evidence—and how strongly do they singly, and much more when combined, affirm the truth of the apostles' testimony. The apostles had "capacity and opportunity for observation" most abundant; they had no possible worldly "interest to pervert the truth;" they have always had the most unimpeached "reputation for veracity;" there is no "conflicting testimony" (though the Jews and the Gentile unbelievers, who have always existed, had the most favorable opportunity, first to collect it, and afterward, from generation to generation, to preserve it, had there been any, against the hated Christians); the evidence has much that is "corroborative and cumulative;" and, finally, all the preceding (as we shall see farther on), contemporaneous, and succeeding, circumstances, are in entire harmony with it. Indeed, the succeeding history of the world—the success of Christianity, and the great changes it caused in the nations—cannot otherwise be explained; and all this occurred too, not in an age, or among a nation, too remote from intelligence and civilization for us to have any sufficient light by which to judge of their reality, but in the most enlightened age of ancient times, and concerning whose transactions we have the fullest history.

Still more, consider these farther laws of evidence which, in justice, we must always observe in estimating whether a witness is guilty of falsehood. "Where a criminal charge is to be proved by circumstantial evidence [as must be in convicting the apostles of false witness], the proof ought to be not only consistent with the prisoner's guilt, but *inconsistent with every other rational conclusion.* This presumption is so strong, that where the guilt can be established only by proving a negative, that negative must in most cases be proved by the party alleging the guilt, though the general rule of law devolves the burden of proof on the party holding the affirmation" (Greenleaf's "Evidence," Ch. iv., Secs. 34, 35). Again (*vide id.*), it is universally admitted that, in proving a case, it is sufficient to prove it in "substance," and that declarations against temporal interests, dying declarations, preceding confirmatory testimony, subjection to cross-examination, and admissions from the silence of opposers, are all to have great weight toward establishing a fact. But all these marks the apostles' testimony had. They all, nevertheless, testify in "substance," to say the least, to the same facts; and any denial, on any hypothesis, of its truth, instead of being so "consistent with their guilt, and inconsistent with every other hypothesis," as to overthrow the presumption of their innocence, has always actually been found to be consistent with nothing, and inconsistent with all the circumstances of the time and place.

We must assent to the absolute truth of the facts recounted in the Gospel histories. And this, with the preceding chapters, finishes the first part of our work by establishing the full admissibility of the evidence presented in those histories in proof of the divinity of Christianity, and brings us next to consider the weight of that evidence for that end. That consideration will occupy the Second Part of this work, to which the reader's sincere attention will then be invited.

Previous to this, however, we will briefly show also that we have substantially the same accounts which those authors originally gave. This is proved by the collation of the Scripture citations made by the various authors already referred to, both friends and opponents, by the comparison of the versions in the different languages, but especially by that of the many ancient manuscripts existing of the New Testament. Indeed, the reverence in which these sacred books were held, the great care used to keep them uncorrupted, the denunciations made in themselves against all who should either "add any thing to," or "take any thing away, from the words written" therein, would lead us to expect no substantial alteration. And, in point of fact, on comparison of all those citations, all the various translations and manuscripts, the latter amounting to thousands in number, though originally widely scattered over Europe, Asia, and Africa, and guarded by extreme care and reverence, as also by the rival jealousies of different nations and the different sects into which the Church was early divided, we yet find no substantial disagreement. In each individual manuscript, indeed, are to be found mistakes proceeding from negligence, ignorance, or unavoidable error in the copyist, who had always to laboriously transcribe by hand. These are such as the following, viz.: Sometimes substituting other words or letters in various places; omitting, adding, or transposing words; incorporating notes and comments found on the margin of the copy before them; in endeavoring to correct supposed errors therein; and rarely through manifestly willful corruption. But all, or nearly all, of these variations are slight and unimportant, and make no material difference in the meaning of the text. Such are—as in John i. 1, "The Word was *in* God," for "*with* God;" verse 3, "In him *is* life," for "was life;" verse 5, "The darkness comprehended *him* not," for "it not;" verse 7, omitting "That all men might believe through him;" verse 9, "That cometh into *this* world," for "*the* world." Many are even slighter than these, and cannot be made apparent in translation. Moreover, they are not all found in any one manuscript; and thus we can correct the errors in one by the agreement found as to that particular part in the great mass of the other MSS., as well as the other versions and citations.

On the other hand, the very fact of these variations existing in the various versions MSS., and citations, prove conclusively that there could have been no agreement to forge between their authors, and therefore that they wrote independently of each other. But since they, nevertheless, substantially agree, we have in this the very strongest proof, both of the genuineness and the uncorrupted preservation of the Scriptures; and this evidence is the greater, the larger the number of citations, versions, and MSS., we have to compare, of the last of which there are thousands.

PART SECOND.

The Weight of the Evidence — The Superhuman Facts.

CHAPTER I.

THE SUPERHUMAN ADVENT OF CHRIST.

We now come to consider the weight of the evidence in favor of the divinity of Christianity. In doing so, we naturally turn, first, to those great facts of Christ's history, attested by the Gospels, which form the indispensable foundation of Christianity, and which, we allege, are not only true, but superhuman and divine. Now, fairly and fully to determine the real origin and character of any action or event, it is manifestly proper to examine, to the best of our ability, not only the circumstances of its rise, but also its essential nature, its agreement in principle with other things known to proceed from the same author from which it professes to have come, and, lastly, its practical influence and tendency in the results that have followed its occurrence in the world. For instance, if a written document—

a poem, a mathematical paper, or a business agreement—were presented to us as the work of some eminent man, if its genuineness were questioned, we ought to examine, first, whether its internal character — in language and sentiment, in mathematical attainments, or in the business skill evident—is such as it is reasonable to expect from such a poet, mathematician, or business man, as the person whose production it is asserted to be. But, to test its genuineness thoroughly, we should not stop here, but proceed farther to compare the handwriting, so far as we were able, with that of other documents known to be genuine. Farther, we should inquire what verdict other men, who have investigated the subject, have given, and, lastly, we should ask whether it has actually accomplished such results in the world, as such a document, by such a man, would reasonably be expected to produce. By these inquiries we should scarcely fail of detecting the forgery that professed to be a poem by Shakespeare, a scientific work by Newton, or an important paper by some great statesman, as Jefferson or Pitt; and these would comprise all the questions which could arise in any discussion of its genuineness. So in our examination of the Evidences of Christianity. The Christian Religion does not shrink from the most thorough investigation; nay, she courts it, and calls loudly, but often in vain, for an inquiry into her claims—and that by the application of all the tests of truth that are in the nature of the case possible—securely confident that a candid and thorough inspection will find fresh evidence on every side that she is truly divine. Accordingly, we will endeavor to consider her claims in all their aspects, and take up, first, the superhuman and divine character of the facts presented in the history of Christ (1. The Superhuman Facts); secondly, the superhuman and divine character of the results produced in the world by Christianity (2. The Superhuman Results); and, thirdly, conclude with a recapitulation and summing up of the whole evidence and argument, and with an estimation of its weight in favor of the divinity of the Christian religion (3. Recapitulation and Conclusion).

First, then, let us consider the superhuman facts. Under this head are ranged, successively, the superhuman advent, the character, the teaching, the prophecies, and the miracles of Christ. Each of these, it is claimed, proves beyond a reasonable doubt the divinity of Christianity; while all combined, as they are in the evidence of Christianity, together with the proof also afforded by the results following, give an irrefutable and convincing evidence of its divine nature.

In offering that evidence, it is assumed that man is capable of distinguishing what is superhuman and divine. We can reasonably estimate—from history, from observation, and from self-consciousness—what is possible to merely human powers. We can therefore tell what is superhuman, and thus be capable of judging of the divine character of any thing that may be presented to us which claims that character. Besides, as Van Oosterzee truly says ("Dogmatics," p. 124), "If God can give a revelation, he can also, without doubt, make it so plainly recognizable as such that he who receives it will not have the slightest shadow of doubt on this point." Indeed, it cannot be easily imagined that God would create us for his worship, and yet give us no capacity to recognize his voice; nor that in our sore need of a revelation from him, he would leave us without ability to distinguish that revelation, or to know the marks of divinity when they were present. Suffice it to say that the general consent of mankind admits the capacity of human powers to distinguish the divine. At any rate, they who deny the divinity of Christianity, do so since such a denial cannot be made without the implied claim that *they* can distinguish between what is divine and what is not. What they claim for themselves they will probably not deny to others: the friends of Christianity distinctly claim it for all; and therefore we assume that it will not be disputed by any that man has the capacity of recognizing the divine; and we proceed to present the grounds of such a recognition in the Evidences of Christianity.

The consideration, then, that will now engage our attention is the superhuman and divine character of the facts of Christ's personal history; and under this general head, first, the coming of Christ into the world. This, we claim, was in all its circumstances of a character truly superhuman and divine, and proves him to be a Divine Person, that took upon himself also the nature of man. To perceive this, let us consider—

I. *The careful preparation made for the advent of Christ.* The introduction of Christianity (*vide* Van Oosterzee's "Dogmatics," pp. 458–585) was not fortuitous; it did not spring up by chance, and without expectation or design, but after long and careful preparation.

1st. Its announcement is made continually throughout the preceding ages—at first, at the very threshold of the history of fallen man, in the promise given to Adam, that "the seed of the woman shall bruise the serpent's head" (Gen. iii. 15), and repeated in ever clearer terms, successively, to Abraham, "In thy seed shall all the nations of the earth be blessed" (Gen. xxii. 18); to Jacob, "The scepter shall not depart from Judah . . . till Shiloh come" (Gen. xlix. 10); to Moses, "The Lord thy God shall raise up unto thee a Prophet . . . like unto me" (Deut. xviii. 15); and afterward to David, Isaiah, Malachi, etc., through a period of thousands of years. Abraham and his family, also, were set apart from all the nations of the earth, chiefly that there might be "a people prepared for the Lord;" and so, to prepare them, there were given for their discipline—(1) Their slavery in Egypt for four hundred years, which, by its oppressions, put them in opposition to heathendom, both historically and by cultivating in their very hearts an abhorrence of it; (2) the Mosaic system; (3) the reigns of the kings; (4) the sending of the prophets; (5) the coming of the great Forerunner, John the Baptist.

1. In the Mosaic dispensation, "the law was their school-master to bring them to Christ," exciting in them the notion of sin, and an abhorrence of it, through the sacrifices and other ceremonies enjoined. These also had a prophetic meaning, and prefigured Christ, as did

also the whole system of Moses.* Thus contrition for sin was cultivated at the same time with the expectation of redemption among the Jews, while the miraculous deliverances experienced from time to time in their history, by Israel, were intended also to be a revelation to the heathen world (*vide* Ex. xv. 14–16; Deut. ii. 25, etc.) of the existence, omnipotence, and will, of Jehovah. Thus the Mosaic dispensation made ready both Jews and heathen for the coming of Christ.

2. So also with the reigns of the kings. Under them the house of Judah, from which Christ was to arise, is brought forward in the sovereignty of David, and first occupies its leading position, while the existence of the kingdom itself points to the everlasting kingdom of the spiritual Israel and its everlasting King, its glory and dominion to the spiritual conquests of Christ; the Psalms of its great monarch David, meantime, minister to the spiritual elevation of the people, and add striking prophecies of the coming Messiah (*vide* Ps. xvi.; xxii.; xl.; lxix., etc.); and the great temple created by David's son and successor, Sol-

---

* "The entire Old Testament is one great Prediction, one great Type, of Him who should come."—*De Wette* (quoted in Van Oosterzee's "Dogmatics"). Cf. whole Epistle to the Hebrews.

omon, gives emphasis to all. And when at last, in the decline of the kingdom, there came, first the captivity in Babylon, and then the final fall under the Roman power, there was cultivated in the people a longing for that Deliverer who was to come, and for the predicted restoration and triumph of Israel; so that we find in fact, that at the coming of Christ there were holy men and women actually "waiting for the Consolation of Israel."

3. The prophets too, arising in a constant succession, from the time of Samuel to the return from the captivity, by their work in educating the people up to Christianity, directly prepared for the coming of Christ. For this purpose they dwelt upon the *spirituality* of God's law (*vide* Isa. i. 11–18; lviii. 1, etc.), and the *universality* of his kingdom (*vide* Hos. iii. 4, 5; Isa. ii. 2–4, etc.), in contradiction of the formality and intense exclusiveness generally prevalent among the Jews, but in perfect conformity to the gospel of Christ, both in its demands for inward purity and its extension of God's mercy to Gentiles as well as Jews. The prophets also prepared the way, with ever-increasing distinctness, for the acceptance of the true idea of the Messiah to come—of his character, his life, and his work. (Cf., in the order of time in which they were written, Joel ii. 28

–33; Mic. v. 1–4; Isa. vii. 4; ix. 1–6; xi. 1–10; liii.; Jer. xxxi. 30–34; Dan. ii. 44; vii. 13, 14; Zech. vi. 12, 13; ix. 9; Hag. ii. 6–9; Mal. iii. 1–4; v. 6.) Thus the prophecies were, for the contemporaries of the prophets, a source of instruction, comfort, and strength; for the contemporaries of the Lord, the touch-stone by which they could recognize the Christ (*vide* John i. 45); and for the Christian Church they remain a great and enduring proof of the divinity of their religion, and the pledge that its promised salvation also will in the end be fully realized.

4. Finally, the Forerunner, John, who was also the greatest of the prophets, was sent purposely to " prepare the way of the Lord." His character and life are fully attested not only by the Gospels, but also by Josephus, and cannot be doubted; and they were most plainly adapted to effect among the Jews the work of preparation for Christ. The manner of his birth, his unexpected reäppearance after his long-continued silence in the wilderness, and his rigid and austere manner of life, all must have made a deep impression upon all who were " waiting for the Consolation of Israel." His preaching, in its denunciation of the sins of the people, in its announcement of Him that " was to come" and His glory, and, at length, in its directly

pointing out among the people the "Lamb of God," opened the way to thousands to receive Christ; while his baptism of Christ was this public and formal "manifestation" of him to Israel; and afterward, even his premature death, and his influence after death, helped on the work of Christ. (*Vide* Luke vii. 29, 30; Acts xix. 1–6.)

2d. Within heathendom also the work of preparation had been going on. 1. God had already given to the heathen that general revelation which everywhere appears in the works of nature, the teachings of history, and by the inward voice of conscience, testifying, as they do, to the existence of God, his rule, and his justice. The appearance and labors of such great men among them as Pythagoras, Socrates, Plato, Seneca, etc., by which the lessons capable of being drawn forth from those sources were deduced and disseminated, tended unmistakably to bring about not merely a moral but a truly religious civilization, and thus to prepare for Christianity. But the diversity of views which existed among them, their own uncertainty in the most important matters, the incompleteness of the best of their systems, their lack of authority, their inability to adapt their teachings to the capacity of the general mass of men, and the small practical effect of those teachings on the lives of even the philosophers themselves and their few disciples, all called forth a deep longing for superior guidance—for light from above, such as it was evident no philosopher or priest could kindle for the enlightenment of men—and thus again heathendom was prepared for the reception of Christ, the "Light of the world;" and in remarkable accordance with this, we find the traces of an expectation of salvation from the East (cf. Plato, Alcibiades, book 2, and De Repub., II.; the myth of Prometheus; Virgil's Fourth Eclogue; Tacitus, Ann., 5, 13, etc.). 2. Especially by Israel had God prepared the Gentile world. Their wonderful national deliverances, widely known as they were to other nations, and their journeyings (*vide* Ex. xv. 6; Josh. ii. 10; ix. 24); their exile for seventy years in Babylon (*vide* Daniel); the work of some of their prophets in foreign countries (*vide* 1 Kings xvii.; 2 Kings v.; Jonah; Daniel; Jer. xxxvii. 7–9; xxxix. 15–18, etc.); their dispersion into Egypt, Babylon, Syria, Greece, and Rome; above all, their Holy Scriptures, in the Greek translation especially, scattered far and wide over the heathen world—all these had carried the knowledge of the truth throughout the nations, and had prepared them for the coming of Christ. 3. The subjection of a great part of the world to Rome had broken down the walls of separation that had existed between the nations, and thus made it comparatively easy to carry the gospel from land to land. The Greek language, moreover, in which the Gospels were written, had spread over the world, and become a kind of universal language, and thus again the rapid and universal spread of the Scriptures was made easy. So that just at the time when the world, weary and miserable with the ills of the times and the helplessness of humanity, instinctively longed for the Christ, and even looked for the approach from the East, there coincided with them the greatest means and facilities for his coming, and for the propagation of his truth.*

---

*Thus Van Oosterzee, from whom the above is substantially though not altogether literally quoted. So Westcott (Introduction, etc., ch. i.), who still more elaborately presents the same views, in showing how the Jews, by the various changes in their history, had become fitted to propagate a universal gospel, while simultaneous *corresponding* changes in heathendom fitted the heathen nations to receive it, says: "The several phases of partial and independent development were now completed. Judaism had now existed in the face of the most varied nationalities, and had gained an elasticity of shape without losing its distinctness of principle. . . . Conquest swept away gradually the barriers by which the world was divided; . . . the power of paganism everywhere gave way; . . . the old temples were deserted, and the speculations of philosophy had

The "fullness of time" had come, and Christ comes "the center of history, the pivot on which the whole plan of God moves." His greatness, his indispensability to man becomes apparent, while the utter failure of all the greatest of human efforts disposes the nations to embrace him as their only hope.

II. From all this we argue that the advent of Christ was supernatural and divine. We next assert it from the evidence of prophecy. Prophecy is "a miracle of knowledge, and the highest evidence that can be given of a revelation from God" (Horne). If, then, we can show that there were prophecies of the coming of Christ existing long prior to that event, we must admit that his coming had something about it that was supernatural and divine. Such prophecies existed. It is disputed by no one that the whole of the Old Testament existed at least as early as B.C. 265, at or before which time the Greek translation of it, called the Septuagint, was undoubtedly made. But the Old Testament, existing thus at least two and a

---

all led to blank skepticism. . . . But Greece had left a universal literature and language, Rome had founded a universal empire. . . . There was a vague presentiment that a new period was near. . . . And in the East that hope rested. A missionary nation [the Jews] was [thus] waiting to be charged with the heavenly commission, and a world was unconsciously prepared to welcome it."

half centuries—or as long as the first settlement of the United States to the present time—before Christ, contains many predictions of his coming, his character, his life, and his death. In them are predicted some things seemingly very unlikely, and in a complicated and connected series of events. They are, moreover, predicted not all by a single individual, but some by one and some by another prophet—at long intervals of time and place—in a comparatively rude and ignorant age and nation. And they are numerous—so numerous, indeed, that we have not here space to refer even to all, nor to any at length. The following, however, may suffice to show the wonderful nature of these prophecies, fulfilled, as a comparison of the Gospel history will show they were, minutely and exactly so many years afterward. 1. It was predicted (Gen. xlix. 10) that Christ should come before the scepter should "depart from Judah," and (Hag. ii. 6–9; Mal. iii. 1) *before the destruction of the second temple.* And, accordingly, our Lord came just when the Romans did utterly take away the government from the tribe of Judah; and he preached in that temple which about forty years afterward was totally destroyed. 2. It was foretold that he should be born in the town of Bethlehem, and of the tribe of Judah (Micah v. 2); of a virgin (Isa. vii. 14); and of the family of David (Isa. ix. 6, 7; xi. 1, 2). 3. Also, that he would be without outward power or influence to attach the world to himself (Isa. liii. 1–3); and "a stone of stumbling and an offense" (Isa. viii. 14, 15); yet the chief corner-stone of the Church (Isa. xxxviii. 16); and that upon this rock the Jews should fall, and be broken to pieces (Isa. viii. 14, 15). Again, that he should preach the gospel to the poor, instruct the Gentiles, and heal the blind and the sick (Isa. vi. 9–11; xliii. 1, etc.); that he should give himself a ransom for many, be numbered with the transgressors, be mocked, and scorned, and rejected of men, yet make his grave with the rich in his death (Isa. liii.). Moreover, he was not to *lie* in the grave, nor see corruption (Ps. xvi. 10); but to rise again on the third day (Hos. vi. 2; cf. with Matt. xx. 19, etc.); and to ascend into heaven, and there reign at his Father's right-hand with universal dominion (Ps. xvi. 11; lxviii. 18; Isa. ix. 7).

All these were perfectly fulfilled by our Saviour, and he and his apostles continually appealed to their fulfillment, before the unbelieving Jews, as the evidence that he was their promised Messiah. It is evident that if either no such prophecies had before existed among the Jews, or if the facts of his birth, life, and death, had at all deviated from these prophecies, the Jews, those bitter enemies of Christianity, would instantly have exposed the imposture, and at once and forever have silenced its advocates. But they could not, and these wonderful prophecies remain, with their fulfillment, an unanswerable evidence of the superhuman and divine nature of the coming of Christ.

III. His miraculous conception and birth by a virgin attests it. For this great fact we have the evidence not only of the prophecy already cited, and also the testimony of the writers of the New Testament, but still farther the personal testimony of Mary and of Christ. That of Mary was impliedly given, since no contradiction of it by her appears in the Gospels; and, doubtless, given expressly also, since from no one else could the account of the circumstances of his birth at first have become known. And Christ did so testify, not only impliedly, but substantially in express terms, asserting that he "came down from heaven . . . to do the will of Him that sent me" (John vi. 38); that he was "the living Bread which came down from heaven," and asking the unbelieving Jews, "What and if ye shall see the Son of man ascend up where he was before?" (*id.*, vs. 51, 62, etc.). This testimony is of the greatest weight. In fact, if his birth was not thus miraculous, then we must believe, on the other hand—awful conclusion as it is, and such as few infidels even have ever ventured to advance—that Mary was both an impudent, shameless woman, and an author of falsehoods, and that of the most tremendous blasphemy; and that Christ was the son of impurity, and himself an utterer of falsehood and blasphemy. And yet we are to believe that Christ, though of such origin, and nurtured by such a woman, and himself, speaking lies, was yet what he is now, as we shall see, acknowledged by all to have been—the one Perfect Man of all the earth, upon whose unapproachable superiority of life and teaching was founded the Christian Church—incomparably the purest and most powerful agency for good that has ever appeared. In the utter impossibility of this, the only alternative, and in the absence of even the charge of such daring deceit and impiety, on the testimony of the Scriptures, of Mary, and of Christ, the common principles of evidence demand that we admit the fact as proved. And this fact, together with those of the prophecies of, and the preparation made for, the coming of Christ into the world, prove that that coming was in a manner that was truly supernatural and divine.

CHAPTER II.

THE SUPERHUMAN CHARACTER OF CHRIST.

WE next inquire concerning the moral character of Christ, and ask whether it corresponds to such a claim, and possesses such traits, as confirm his divine descent. We expect, if a man claims to be of uncommonly superior origin, to find evidence of the fact not only from the external testimonies he may bring us, but also in the man himself—in his appearance, his manners, his characteristics of mind and disposition. Much more is this the case if he who presents himself before us asserts that he is sprung from a race of beings superior to men —an angel, or from a God. If, on examination of the actions and words narrated of him, we found the same human imperfections as are common to man, we should at once decide that his claim was false. The test is a proper one, and by it we can rightly decide the falsity of the pretensions of all the heroes of the pagan religions (as Hercules, etc.) to divine descent. The histories given of them show them to possess the common frailties of humanity, and in most, if not all, cases to possess also its grossest vices. Probably the inventors of their histories would have made them better if they could; but it is an old observation, illustrated by the literature of every country, that human powers cannot paint a portrait above the human in beauty of moral character. The stream cannot rise above its source; imperfection will cling to this, as to every other work of human skill; without a previous revelation of such a superhuman being, there will have been no model from which to draw; and the authors, though they be the Homers and Virgils of imagination and invention, must leave their heroes marred by many a fault, and even their heavenly gods and goddesses disfigured with many an impurity and imperfection. We have a right, then, to expect, if Christ is divine, that his character and life shall appear, evidently, to be above all that is merely human.

On the other hand, we are just as much bound, in truth and honesty, to acknowledge his divinity if we do find his character thus to be superior to all that is human. The one duty is as clear and obligatory as the other. If the skeptic has the right to demand, for the establishment of Christ's divinity, that we bring forth in proof his possession of a superhuman character, it is surely our right, when that proof has been produced, to demand unhesitating assent to the fact so established by its evidence.

What, then, are the characteristic traits of Christ's moral nature? Are they such as, marked by the imperfections universal to mere human nature, show that he too was no more than man? Or are they free from all blemish? and perfect in nature and in variety of attributes, do they proclaim One who was himself perfect—One far removed above mere imperfect humanity—One who was truly divine? For reply we have the history of his life, given by four different authors, in the Gospels of the New Testament Scriptures. In them his character is simply, but very completely, delineated. He is presented to us under the most trying circumstances conceivable —of the most various kinds, and of the greatest number. The very mission, so unique and so great, which he undertook, at once exposed him to the severest scrutiny, and from its very nature made success to be most difficult to attain. Claiming to be the long-promised Messiah of the Jews, he had to fulfill not only the circumstances of birth, origin, etc., predicted of the Messiah's life, but also the various traits of character foretold of Him that was to come. Claiming to be perfectly holy, he had to exhibit unspotted sanctity of life. Claiming to be divine, he had to display superhuman wisdom, and power, and goodness. Yet the Gospels exhibit him, for more than three years of his life, under the most trying circumstances, wholly unmarred by a single shadow of imperfection. Standing in the most diverse and changing relations with foes and friends, with relatives and strangers, with the common people and the most learned, with Jews and Samaritans, with Greeks, and Romans, and Syrians—in contact with all kinds of life, in the country, the city, the desert, and upon the sea —before the populace and before judges, in peace and in conflict, at rest and at labor, in sorrow and in joy, at the feast and at the burial, in triumph amid the acclamations of the multitude as he entered a King into Jerusalem, and on trial for his life before Caiaphas and before Pilate—ministered to by loving women, and scourged by the soldier's lash—at Bethany and upon Calvary: in all these he is presented to us under almost every conceivable circumstance; and yet, neither when harassed by enemies, nor when relaxed in the presence of ministering and adoring friends, does either his wisdom or his goodness ever forsake him, or betray the faintest sign of any imperfection. Neither vanity on one side, nor bitterness on the other; neither worldly ambition nor any thirst for revenge; no taint of impurity, falsehood, selfishness, or hate, nor, withal, the least diminution of dignity and respect for self, was ever beheld. In all he stood alone; perfect and entire, he towered far above all that is merely human, and remained untouched and unreached by human weakness or human infirmity. He was divine.

To illustrate this by examples drawn from his history would occupy more space than can here be afforded; to fully show it, it would be necessary to consider every incident and all his words and actions, and transcribe, with comments, the whole of the Gospels. Manifestly, nothing like this can be appropriate here. We can only refer the reader to that Life generally, and challenge the severest criticism to find one blemish therein. Hitherto his most acute and bitter enemies have failed to find one; but many, as we shall see, have been forced to testify in his favor. With that fact before us, we add, as sufficient additional proof of what we claim, the following evidence:

1. Man never before even imagined such a character; nor is it possible to imagine one superior. Neither (cf. Rogers's "Supernatural Origin of the Bible") in Greek, nor Roman, nor Jewish, nor any other history or literature, can there be found the elements of another such

character, real or fictitious. Man never has painted, and never can paint, another such a One, by whom the challenge may safely be given, "Which of you convinceth me of sin?" In his practical goodness, in his intellectual greatness, and in his self-abnegation, Christ surpasses all the *ideals* of men, as in his work he has exceeded their greatest heroes in practical importance to the world. In an age of unexampled corruption, a moral standard was erected by One Man—a Jewish peasant, convicted and executed as a felon—which has been unapproached before and since, *and which we cannot even conceive it possible to be excelled*. And still more remarkable, if possible, this has not been in vain, but has been ever since, and still is, the mightiest moral agent for good to be found among men.

2. His divine character is proved from the superhuman influence for good that he has exerted. To quote substantially from Row (Bampton Lectures, 1877), "Present facts, no less than the unquestionable facts of history, prove that Christ stands on an elevation which, among the sons of men, is solitary and alone. Our experience of man, extending over at least three thousand years, with ample opportunity of observation, enables us to know well what is in man, and what man's powers

can accomplish: if therefore the greatness of Christ were the result of their activity, it is clear that during this long interval of time they must have produced other men at least approaching his greatness.

"The life of Christianity consists, most remarkably and absolutely uniquely, in the history of man—not in a body of moral precepts or dogmas, a ritual, or a system of philosophy, but in a personal history. We may take from Brahmanism, Buddhism, Mohammedanism, or any of the philosophical, political, or social systems that have ever existed among men, or from any of the various sects even in the Christian Church, the personal history of their founders, and yet they would remain, substantially unaffected, the same as before. But if from Christianity we take the personal history of Christ, his life, death, and resurrection, we take from it its all. No other system has ever pretended to be founded on a Person, and the events of that Person's life, instead of a body of dogmatic statements. But the supreme attractiveness of the Person of the Founder of Christianity has imparted to the Church the whole of its vitality. To this fact all history bears witness. Nor is its testimony less certain that, of all the influences that have been exerted in this earth, that of Jesus has been the most potent. Enumerate all the great men who have ever existed, whether they be kings, conquerors, statesmen, poets, philosophers, or men of science, and their influence for good will be found to be as nothing compared with that which has been exerted by Jesus Christ.* . . . He who was in outward form a Galilean peasant, who died a malefactor's death, has founded a spiritual empire which has endured for eighteen centuries of time, and which, despite the vaticination of unbelievers, shows no sign of decrepitude. Commencing with the smallest beginnings, his empire now embraces all the progressive races of men. Those by whom it has not been accepted are in a state of stagnation and decay. It is the only one which is adapted to every state of civilization. It differs from all other states and communities in that it is founded neither on force nor self-interest, but on persuasion and the supreme attractiveness of the character of its Founder. The holiest of men have bowed before him with the supremest reverence, and have accepted him as a King

---

* The acknowledgment of Napoleon, on St. Helena, will here be remembered, when, comparing the littleness of his own dominion, already past, and those also of Alexander, Cæsar, etc., with the wide extension and durability of that of Christ, he declared that Christ alone was divine.

who is entitled to reign by right of inherent worthiness, and with the greater eagerness in proportion to their holiness" (pp. 93, 94).

3. We farther adduce the testimony of his opposers. The one catholic man, the one ideal of humanity, even his enemies are forced to praise him. The skeptical historian, Lecky ("History of Morals," Vol. II., ch. 8), says: "It was reserved for Christianity to present to the world an ideal character which, through all the changes of eighteen centuries, has filled the hearts of men with an impassioned love, and has shown itself capable of acting on all ages, nations, temperaments, and conditions; has not only been the highest pattern of virtue, but the highest incentive to its practice, and has exerted so deep an influence that it may be truly said that the simple record of three short years of active life has done more to regenerate and to soften mankind than all the disquisitions of philosophers, and than all the exhortations of moralists. This has indeed been the well-spring of whatever has been best and purest in the Christian life. Amid all the sins and failings, amid all the priestcraft, the persecution, and fanaticism which have defaced Christianity, it has preserved in the character and the example of its Founder an enduring principle of regeneration."

But, argues Row, what other character, real or ideal, among men, has (1) "for eighteen centuries filled the hearts of men with an impassioned love?" Has Socrates, Zoroaster, or Mohammed? or any ideal character, even the greatest, of Homer, or Virgil, or Shakespeare? (2) What other has thus "acted on all ages, nations, and temperaments?" Has Shakespeare? Who is impelled to self-sacrifice for the love of Shakespeare? (3) Or, who else has "presented the highest pattern of virtue?" (4) Or, in himself is "the highest incentive to its practice?" (5) Or, has ever been "an enduring principle of regeneration" to his system? Has any heathen? any apostle even? or any Father of the Church? Nay, Christ alone has been able to accomplish such things. All others, even the very best, of all ages and nations together, have not been able to equal him. Can it be doubted that he is divine?

Again, "In Christ," says Chubb, an avowed infidel, "we have an example of a quiet and peaceable spirit, just, honest, upright, and sincere, and, above all, of a most gracious temper and behavior—one who did no injury to any man, in whose mouth there was no guile, who went about doing good. His life was a beautiful picture of human nature in its native purity and simplicity, and showed at once what excellent creatures men would be when under the influence and power of that gospel which he preached unto them." Again, Rousseau exclaims, "What sweetness, what purity in his manners! What an affecting gracefulness in his delivery! What sublimity in his maxims! What profound wisdom in his discourses! What presence of mind in his replies! How great the command over the passions! Where is the man, where is the philosopher, who could so live and so die without weakness and without ostentation? . . . Shall we suppose the evangelic history a mere fiction? Indeed, my friend, it bears not the marks of fiction. On the contrary, the history of Socrates, which nobody presumes to doubt, is not so well attested as that of Jesus Christ. Such a supposition, in fact, only shifts the difficulty without removing it; for it is more inconceivable that a number of persons should agree to write such a history than that only one should furnish the subject of it. The Jewish authors were incapable of the diction, and were strangers to the morality, contained in the gospel, the marks of whose truth are so striking and inimitable that the inventor would be a more astonishing character than the hero." Finally, we add the testimony of one of the most intellectual of unbelievers,

John Stuart Mill. He says ("Three Essays"), "It is the God Incarnate more than the God of the Jews who, being idealized, has taken so great and salutary a hold on the modern mind. And whatever else may be taken away from us by rational criticism, Christ is still left—a unique figure not more unlike all his predecessors than all his followers."

Such testimony from witnesses so incapable of partiality toward Christianity, and so capable intellectually of correct judgment, could have been called forth only by the superhuman and irresistible beauty and grandeur of the character of Christ. In itself it is a strong proof of his divinity, and, together with the preceding evidences to the same fact, is a sufficient proof. "The forces which energize in the moral and spiritual world act in conformity with the moral laws no less than those which dominate in the physical universe do with physical laws; and therefore an event in the moral universe, of the origin of which the forces energizing in man can give no account, is a moral miracle."—*Row*. We know from universal history and literature what the "forces energizing in man" can produce of human character and human life; we have seen how impossible it is for them to produce such another character and life as that of Christ; and we must conclude, therefore, that his appearance upon the stage of human history was "an event in the moral universe, of the origin of which the forces energizing in man can give no account"—"a moral miracle"—and proves him to be superhuman and divine.

This might be justly thought to be sufficient; but we farther cite, in connection with this subject—

4. The testimony of Christ to himself. In doing this, we violate no rule of evidence. His enemies being judges, we have found him to be irreproachably holy, supremely great, and spotlessly true. His testimony, then, is worthy to be received, and to be fully credited. Besides, such evidence is now everywhere admitted. By a late and very proper change in jurisprudence (cf. *Princeton Review*, July, 1878, p. 154, etc.), the testimony of parties in interest is now generally received. The weight of their testimony is left to be decided according to each one's credibility, his disinterestedness, conscientiousness, and intellectual ability; and this is felt to be right, inasmuch as otherwise the very parties who alone could know best about the matter in question, though of the highest integrity, are excluded.

But it is allowed on all hands, as we have seen, that Christ, in all the qualities of greatness of intellect, perfect uprightness of life, and purity of heart, is wholly unapproached by any other who has ever lived on earth. His testimony, then, upon the common principles of evidence, though given in reference to himself, his divine origin, and his mission, is entitled to the very greatest weight. As such we cite it in support of his divinity, and ask candid attention to the following, among others, of his words and acts:

1. He acquiesced without denial in Nicodemus's declaration, that he was "a teacher come from God" (John iii. 2); 2. He directly declared to the Samaritan woman that he was "Messias" (John iv. 26); 3. He "made himself equal with God" (John vi. 35, 38); 4. He asserted that he had "come down from heaven" (John vi. 35, 38); 5. That he was the source of everlasting life to men (John vi. 47–56); 6. He assented to the declaration that he was "Christ the Son of the living God" (John vi. 68, 69); 7. And declared that he "proceedeth forth, and came from God" (John viii. 42); 8. And that "before Abraham was, I am" (John viii. 58); 9. That "I and my Father are one," and "the Father is in me, and I in him"(John x. 30, 38); "As the Father knoweth me, even so know I the Father" (John x. 15); and "*I* give unto them eternal life" (John x. 28); 10.

He "knew that he was come from God, and went to God" (John xiii. 3); 11. Commanded his disciples, "Ye believe in God, believe also in me" (John xiv. 1); 12. Said that "he that hath seen me hath seen the Father" (John xiv. 9); 13. Acknowledged himself to be the "Son of God" (Luke xxii. 70; cf. also parallel passages); 14. And said to the disciples, "*Receive ye the Holy Ghost*," at the same time breathing upon them, and imparting him to them.

This and such like testimony he repeatedly gave of himself. Now, either he was willfully a false witness, or mistaken, or else his testimony was true. If false, then was he the most awfully perjured and blasphemous man, and the most injurious to his race of all that have ever lived; if mistaken, then the most deceived. But we see that even unbelievers acknowledge him to be, far above all comparison, both the most profound in intellect and the most holy in life of all men. The only rational explanation, then, of his testimony—the only possible solution consistent both with his character and with all the circumstances of his life —is that it was true, and that he was really divine; and we therefore add this evidence of his own testimony of himself, to prove what we claim for him—that in his very character he also evidently appears to be divine.

CHAPTER III.

THE SUPERHUMAN TEACHING OF CHRIST—I.
ITS REASONABLENESS.

NEXT we call attention to the teaching of Christ, as exhibiting, in its unrivaled wisdom, fullness, and power, a character utterly unknown to that of any other teacher that has ever appeared—proving thereby that it is more than human, and is, as it claims to be, divine. We have already seen, in the First Part of this work, how confessedly imperfect and unsatisfying have been the reasonings of all, even the greatest of, merely human moralists and philosophers. In the most striking contrast stands the teaching of Jesus of Nazareth. "Never man spake like this man." There is nowhere any appearance or shadow of folly or mistake, but always the profoundest wisdom. There is nowhere any incompleteness or uncertainty, but in every thing unfathomable fullness, perfect sufficiency, and the most confident assurance; and among no people, with no class of men or women, and under no circumstances of life, whether of age or youth, of adversity or prosperity, of barbarism or of the highest and most complicated civilization, has his teaching ever ceased to exercise, through all the centuries since first it was given to the world, its wonderful power to elevate and ennoble the human-heart.

"A hundred years ago a distinguished company of eminent men was assembled in a drawing-room in Paris. Again, as it was customary in that circle, Holy Scripture had been the general drudge; from all sides the sharp and envenomed arrows of mockery were aimed at it. At once one of the boldest among these free-thinkers—the famous Diderot—rose from his seat, and, to the general amazement of the company, said: 'All right, gentlemen, all right! I am ready to declare all of you clever writers and competent judges, and few in France or abroad would be able to speak or write better than you do. But still, notwithstanding all the evil we have just been saying about this accursed Book, and which, no doubt, serves it right, still I think I might defy any of you to compose an historical tale so ingenious, and at the same time so sublime, so touching, and fit to produce such a deep and lasting influence for centuries to come, as the Gospel relation of Christ's sufferings and death.' No wonder an unwonted but most significant silence followed." This story—given by Van Oosterzee, in an article in the *Princeton Review* of July, 1878, the truth of which there seems no reason to doubt—serves to bring out in measurable relief the superhuman character of the Gospels. For what author has ever written, or will dare to pretend he could write, any history rivaling it? But what is beyond human achievement is superhuman, and therefore we claim that the gospel is divine.

To prove this at large, let us compare the main teachings of Christianity, first with those of the leading philosophers both of ancient and modern times, and next with the known constitution and course of nature, manifested in the ordinary course of things in the world around us. In their agreement with both of these, we shall see their entire reasonableness; in their analogy to the latter, we shall behold the evidence that the same all-wise and all-powerful Creator, who is nature's Maker, is also the Author of Christianity; and in their incomparable superiority to the teachings of both philosophers and nature, we shall see that they are superhuman and divine.

I. A sufficient view (Part I., Ch. 3) of the defects and vices of all the schemes of the philosophers has already been shown. No such imperfections have ever been pointed out in the teachings of Christ; and from this single superiority of being free from the human infirmity everywhere else apparent, we might justly claim that it is divine. But this is still more strikingly apparent in the superiority it manifests when compared, not with the defects, but with the best achievements of their reasonings. To show that it does possess such a superiority is not difficult, and to do so will be our duty before leaving this part of our general subject. First, however, it is proper to show that Christianity is in entire agreement with reason and nature, and therefore consistent with divine wisdom; afterward we shall consider its superiority to both.

The agreement of the doctrines taught by Christ with reason is proved by their accordance with the conclusions of the greatest reasoners, both ancient and modern, that have ever lived. To see this distinctly, let us briefly recall what are the principal truths that were taught by Christ.

These may be stated to consist in: 1. The unity of God. 2. The depravity of man. 3. The immortality of the soul; together with the following, given by Coleridge ("Aids to Reflection," p. 146), as peculiar to Christianity alone, viz.: 4. "That a mean of salvation has been effected and provided for the human race by the incarnation of the Son of God in the person of Jesus Christ, and that his life on earth, his sufferings, death, and resurrection, are not only proofs and manifestations, but likewise essential and effective parts, of the great redemptive act, whereby also the obstacle from the corruption of our nature is rendered no longer insurmountable. 5. That the appropriation of this benefit is possible by repentance and faith, including the aids that render an effective faith and repentance themselves possible. 6. That there is a reception (by as many as *shall be heirs of salvation*) of a living and spiritual principle, a seed of life, capable of surviving this natural life, and of existing in a divine and immortal state. 7. That there is an awakening of the spirit in them that truly believe, and a communion of that spirit thus awakened with the Holy Spirit. 8. That there are accompanying and consequent gifts, graces, comforts, and privileges of the Spirit, which, acting primarily of the heart and will, cannot but manifest themselves in suitable works of love and obedience—that is, in right acts, with right affections, from right principles. 9. That these works are the appointed signs and evidences of our faith, and that, under limitation of the powers, the means, and the opportunities afforded us individually, they are the rule and measure by which we are bound and enabled to judge of *what spirit we are.* 10. That God beholds us, and will finally judge us with a merciful consideration of our infirmities, a gracious acceptance of our sincere though imperfect strivings, and a forgiveness of our defects, through the mediation of the man Christ Jesus, even the Word, that was in the beginning with God, and who, being God, became [also] man for the redemption of mankind."

1st. That the doctrines of Christianity are reasonable, appears from their very nature. "This world [*vide* Wayland's "Moral Science"] is a universe governed by law; if by physical laws, then by moral law also, since the world of morals has its existence and laws in the universe as well as the physical world. Their violation, then, must as certainly be visited with retribution as that of physical laws, sometime and somehow. Therefore, since such retribution often does not happen here, it must hereafter; therefore there is a future life, and that life is retributive." Again, "The obligation of supreme love to God is reasonable: 1. He is our Creator and Preserver. 2. He unites within himself every perfection that can possibly exist. 3. His creative power and his infinite wisdom have been exerted for the production of our best good. 4. Therefore he has the right over us of unlimited possession.

5. And of our highest love and gratitude. 6. Therefore, since the universe is governed by law, we can attain happiness only by discharging those obligations (since the violation of every law or duty is attended with punishment). 7. Or mutually render each other happy, since to do so it is necessary for all to be under the control of a supreme Power, and to fulfill the law of love to each other.

"The duty of prayer also is evident. For, 1. We are powerless, ignorant of the future, dependent, and miserably sinful. 2. We continually receive blessings from God, to whom we should also render continual thanks. 3. Its exercise is necessary to our well-being here, since the temper and frame of mind (as penitence, faith, devotion, etc.) it must imply and exercise is essential to our progress in virtue. Those of benevolence, of justice, of truth, of chastity, and of filial obedience, are no less apparent; while those also of the Sabbath, of hearing the word of God, of public worship, etc., are not difficult to be seen."

This reasoning, drawn from a modern moralist, to whose conclusions, however, no one without the light of revelation ever attained with any certainty, fullness, or consistency, shows the reasonableness of Christianity in the nature of the case itself.

2d. The agreement of the deductions of some of the greatest intellects of the human race with the doctrines of Christianity show that the latter are not contrary to reason, but wholly reasonable, and worthy of our acceptance. From among the many illustrious thinkers who might be brought forward to prove, by their writings, this agreement, our space permits us here to cite only those that are greatest—Plato and Aristotle among the ancients, and Descartes, Locke, and Hunt, among the moderns.

1. Plato teaches (*vide* Ueberweg's "History of Philosophy," sections 41 and 43) that "The highest object of knowledge is *the Idea of the Good*. This Idea is supreme, and the cause of all truth and beauty. Every thing which exists, and is knowable, has received from God, *who is the Idea of the Good*, its existence and ability to be known, because he knew that it was better that it should exist than that it should not exist." He also teaches that the world must have had a beginning (*vide* Tim., pages 28, 29): "God's goodness is the reason of the construction of the world, and being therefore without envy, he planned all things so that they should be as nearly as possible like himself." The soul is immortal; the highest good is not pleasure, nor knowledge alone,

but the *greatest possible likeness to God*, as the absolutely good; and the possession of that good is happiness. Most striking is the resemblance of the picture he draws of the purely righteous to the character and life of our Lord (De Repub., 360, 361): "He has the ring of Gyges, that gives invisibility; he has power to do all evil with impunity and without reproach, yet is he righteous still. He may have the very opposite of this impunity, but unjustly receive the reputation of unrighteousness, and with no means of reversing the unjust decision, yet is he righteous still. He may be made to endure the severest pains with no prospect of deliverance, either now or at any other time, yet is he righteous still. Finally, what may such a man, in such circumstances, expect from his fellow-man? 'The righteous man, in this state, will be scourged, he will suffer dislocating tortures, he shall be bound with cords, and finally, after suffering all evils, *shall be impaled, or crucified.*'" Compare only these wonderful utterances of what this master-mind conceived to be required by true reason with the teachings of the Bible as to the character and attributes of God, the nature of man, and the true end of life, together with its account of the actual life of Christ as the ideal man, and how well satisfied may we be that Christianity, both as to its doctrines and as to the facts of the life upon which it founds its hopes, is entirely consistent with the demands of the highest reason.

2. The like truth is shown also by what Aristotle, the great opponent of Plato's system in general, deduced as the necessary conclusions of reason (Ueberweg, secs. 48–50): "In the sphere of existence we find included that which is perpetually moved, and that which both moves and is moved; there exists therefore a third existence, which is always imparting motion, but is itself unmoved. This is God, *the immaterial and eternal Form, the pure Actuality, in which is no potentiality, the self-thinking Reason, or absolute Spirit, who, as absolutely perfect, is loved by all, and into the image of whose perfection all things seek to come.* He occupies the very highest place in the scale of being, is without parts, is the Good; not a final product of development, but *the eternal* PRIUS *of all development.* The highest good for man is happiness. This depends on the rational or virtuous activity of the soul throughout the whole of its life. The highest among the virtues is justice, or righteousness. Man's only worthy activity is honorable and virtuous activity, and the highest happiness is connected with the highest virtue." Such are the de-

ductions of these two ancient masters, in perfect conformity (except their opposite ideas of the chief good of man, which, however, is of small moment, since both make virtue and happiness inseparable) with each other and with the truths of revelation. Let us now turn to the moderns.

3. We first take Descartes, the father of modern philosophy (Ueberweg, sec. 114): "He seeks to demonstrate the existence of God and the existence of the soul as an independent entity, separable from the body. . . There must be a first cause, which is God, and among the necessary attributes of God belongs the love of truth. God cannot wish to deceive," hence clear and distinct knowledge is attainable by man. "God is the absolutely perfect being. In the conception of God there is contained necessary, perfect, and eternal existence. Only one substance can be conceived as plainly needing nothing else in order to its existence, namely, God, for we plainly perceive that all others cannot exist without God's assistance. He attributes to matter nothing but extension and modes of extension, but no internal states, or forces. Pressure and impulsion (coming from God), the sum of which, in the universe, is invariable, must suffice for the explanation of all phenomena. The most per-

fect of all emotions is intellectual love to God. Virtue depends on the control of the passions by wisdom."

4. Of Locke, the great antagonist of, and founder of the school of philosophy opposed to, Descartes, it is scarcely necessary to speak to English readers as a devout believer and defender of Christianity. He held, it is true, that the immortality of the soul could not be *demonstrated*, by human reason, but was a subject for revelation only; but he found no contradiction to reason in the doctrine; while the existence of God, his essential, original, omnipresent, and eternal being, the cause of all other things, and the foundation of all morality, he thought were clearly proved by reason (*vide* "Human Understanding"). So also in his work, "Reasonableness of Christianity," he specifically maintains the reasonable nature of the essential doctrine of the Christian belief —viz., salvation by faith in our Lord Jesus Christ—and he continued through life a sincere and consistent professor of that faith.

5. Leibnitz, who, Ueberweg says (sec. 117), was "the founder of the German philosophy of the eighteenth century," finds that God exists, and is "the most perfect Being, than whom no greater can be conceived. The good man is he who loves all men, so far as reason

permits, and justice is the virtue which controls this love. Submission to the eternal laws of the Divine Monarchy is justice in the universal sense, in which it includes all virtues in itself. The particular phenomena of nature can and must be mechanically explained; but the principles of physics and mechanics themselves depend on the direction of a Supreme Intelligence, and can only be explained when we take into consideration this Intelligence; therefore, the true principles of physics must be deduced from the divine perfections. The soul governs the body, and from its unity and spirituality he infers its indestructibility and immortality. God is the primitive Unity, or the original, simple, and absolute Substance. He has an adequate knowledge of all things, since he is the Source of all; is an omnipresent Center, and all things are immediately present to him. God governs nature as its Architect, the world of spirits as their Monarch; and between the kingdoms of nature and grace there is a predetermined harmony. As to moral evil, or wrong, God could not remove them without removing the power of self-determination, and therewith the possibility of morality itself; therefore, freedom, not as exemption from law, but as the power of deciding for one's self according to known law, belongs to the essence of the human spirit. The course of nature is so ordered by God as in all cases to accord with the highest interests of the soul; and in this consists the harmony between the kingdoms of nature and grace."

6. Finally, we cite Kant, the illustrious metaphysician of Germany, perhaps both the most comprehensive and profound of all modern philosophers. "Pure reason," he teaches, "demands the doctrines of the freedom of the will, the immortality of the human soul, and the existence of God. The moral law requires holiness—*i. e.*, perfect conformity of the will to the moral law. But the consciousness of a continual bent toward transgression, or at least toward impurity of motive—*i. e.*, toward the intermixture of imperfect, non-moral motives of obedience—accompanies the spirit in its best estate. Virtue is the *highest* good, happiness the indispensable condition of the realization of perfect good." In his work entitled "Religion Within the Limits of Mere Reason," he teaches, in its four parts, of—"1. The indwelling of an evil principle, side by side with the good one, in human nature, or of the radical evil in human nature; 2. Of the contest between the good and evil principles for the control of man; 3. Of the victory of the good principle over the evil one, and of the founda-

tion of a kingdom of God on the earth; 4. Of true and false religious service under the rule of the good principle, or of religion and priestcraft. There is in human nature a propensity to reverse the moral order. The good principle is humanity in its complete moral perfection (of which happiness is, by the will of the Supreme Being, the immediate consequence). Man, thus conceived—and only thus is he well-pleasing to God—may be represented as the Son of God. In practical faith on this Son of God, man may hope to become well-pleasing to God, and so to attain to blessedness; or, in other words, that man is not an unworthy object of the divine complacency who is conscious of such a moral disposition that he can believe, with a well-grounded confidence in himself, that, if subjected to temptations and sufferings like those which (in the gospel of Christ) are made the touch-stone of the ideal of humanity, he would remain unalterably loyal to that ideal, faithfully following it as his model, and retaining its likeness."

Such are the conclusions of the protracted and profound meditations of these intellectual giants. They cannot, of course, be made to give evidence as to those doctrines of Christianity—as, *e. g.*, the incarnation, the sufficiency of the atonement, the resurrection, etc.

—which from their very nature are necessarily the subject of revelation only. But upon nearly, if not all, those that are capable of the deductions of unaided reason—those of the depravity of human nature, the existence and nature of God, the obligation of his law, the nature and the necessity of holiness, the immortality of the soul, the reasonableness of requiring faith for salvation, etc.—in such as these, their conclusions, arrived at in some points by one, in others by another, show the agreement of Christianity with reason. No one, indeed, of those great intellects was ever able singly to ascertain all these great truths without the aid of revelation; with much that is good the most eminent of them, unlike Christ, have mingled much that was unworthy; and, at the best, their conclusions fall far short of the sublimity, the purity, the consistency, and the certainty, of Bible doctrine. Yet, when we find the greatest minds of all ages, though totally differing in their methods and as to many of their principles, nevertheless sustaining, some one, some another, of the doctrines of the Bible, we must conclude that Christianity is at least not unreasonable; and farther, even as to those doctrines which cannot without revelation be made the subject of reasoning, yet, when revealed, there has never been proved any disagreement between them and reason. Finally, when we consider how many of the most distinguished leaders of human thought, in various fields of knowledge, have given in their adhesion not only to those doctrines in some measure deducible by reason, but also to those which must be given by revelation alone, our conclusion is still farther strengthened. Poets like Shakespeare, Milton, and Tennyson; statesmen like Pitt, and Gladstone, and Webster, and Calhoun; mental philosophers like Sir William Hamilton, Coleridge, and Dugald Stewart; physicists like Newton and Davy, like Faraday, Agassiz, and Maury—have fully believed in the truth of Christianity. It is almost impossible that any set of principles thus concurred in by so many of the greatest intellects, looking from such various stand-points of pursuit and of historical period, etc., can be unreasonable and absurd. The objection that is sometimes urged, on the ground of the mysterious nature of some of the peculiar doctrines of Christianity, is easily answered. If we are to receive that religion only that is without mystery, and to which our reason is adequate, then we must reject all religion whatsoever. For every religion must suppose a God; yet the nature and the mode of existence of God is wholly mysterious to us, and lies beyond our reason. Nay, if we receive nothing but what is fully explainable to us, we must reject all sciences and arts, and, what is more, the notion we have of our own existence; for all of these involve principles not capable of being understood by us.*

---

*The absurdity of this objection is well shown by the following illustration, taken from Coleridge: "A sick man, whose complaint was as obscure as his sufferings were severe and notorious, was thus addressed by a humane stranger: 'My poor friend, I find you dangerously ill, and on this account only, and because you have not wherewith to pay a physician, I have come to you. Respecting your disease, indeed, I can tell you nothing that you are capable of understanding, more than you already know, or can be taught by reflection on your own experience. But I have rendered the disease no longer irremediable. I have brought the remedy with me, and I now offer the means of immediate relief to you, with the assurance of convalescence and a final perfect cure — nothing more being required on your part but your best endeavors to follow the prescriptions I shall leave with you. Ask not how such a disease is possible; enough for the present that you know it to be real. I come to cure the disease, not to explain it.'" ("Aids to Reflection," p. 221.) What would be thought of the patient's objecting to the efficiency of the remedy because he did not understand its manner of operation? "But if thou canst not read the mystery of birds," says Cyril, "when soaring on high, how wouldest thou read the Maker of things? Who among men knows even the names of all wild beasts? or who can accurately classify their natures? But if we know not even their bare names, how should we comprehend their Maker?"

Christianity, then, loses nothing in its claim to be reasonable because in some things it is mysterious to us. There is nothing in it *contrary* to reason, and that it has much that is above reason is surely no just ground of objection to its divine character; nay, we expect to find in that which is divine something beyond the grasp of human powers, and we would justly at once disbelieve in its divinity did we *not* find in it something that was incomprehensible to us.

CHAPTER IV.

THE SUPERHUMAN TEACHING OF CHRIST—II. THE ANALOGY OF NATURE—III. ITS SUPERIORITY BOTH TO HUMAN REASON AND NATURE.

II. We are next to show that the principles of Christianity are in harmony with the well-known constitution and course of nature about us. This agreement, it is claimed, is so general and remarkable, in the nature as well of the *difficulties* as of the things not difficult, contained in each, as to constitute an analogy, or likeness, and thus to show unmistakably that both are from the hand of the same author, even God. The argument following, in proof of this position, is taken from Butler's celebrated work, the "Analogy of Religion"—an argument which, so far as the author is aware, no skeptic has ever even ventured to attack, and which certainly no one has ever attacked with success. In following it, we find it indicated by nature.

1. That mankind is appointed to live in a future state. For (1) it is a general law of nature that all creatures should exist in various stages of life, under greatly changed

conditions and states of life. Thus the life of a man, from the state of life in the womb before birth to that of his fully-developed powers of manhood, passes through various exceedingly different states and conditions, equally with that of the butterfly from the worm to the gay and fully-developed insect. Therefore, that we are to exist hereafter in a state as different from this our present state of existence as this is from our former condition, is not against, but according to, the analogy of nature. (2) The possession of our living powers of action and feeling now is a presumption that they will still exist hereafter. Continuance is the law of all being—*i. e.*, of all those qualities necessary to *existence* (cf. the scientific principle of continuity set forth in "The Unseen Universe"). Therefore, unless some reason can be shown why death should destroy them, we must presume that our powers of action and feeling will continue, in some state, to exist. But there is no ground to believe that death will destroy them. The mere cessation of their exercise does not prove their destruction, for their exercise is suspended also in sleep, and in a swoon, yet not destroyed. The body, as a whole, appears to be in this respect just like each of its parts—the eye, or the hand—merely the instrument of the inward powers of the mind, and just as any one part —the eye, or the hand—may perish, and yet leave those mental powers themselves entirely unimpaired, so may the whole body perish, and leave them unimpaired. On the contrary, since it is manifest that our gross body is not necessary to our intellectual enjoyments; since, indeed, it often leaves them wholly unimpaired, though it is reduced to the extremity of weakness, and to the verge of death; there is no ground therefore, in nature, for believing that the exercise of our faculties is at all *suspended*, even by death itself. Death, on the contrary, may in some sort answer to our birth, and, like it, put us into a higher and more enlarged state of life. As death therefore does not appear likely to destroy us, it is probable we shall live on, and the next life may be as *natural* as the present.

2. Nature teaches us that in that future state men shall be rewarded good or evil, as they have been virtuous or vicious here. (1) We find, in general, that in nature pain follows vice, and happiness results from virtue; and moreover, as with intemperance, that such pain often follows actions which are accompanied with much present pleasure. (2) That it is often much greater than the pleasure. (3) Its delay is no presumption of final impunity. (4)

After such delay they often come suddenly. (5) And that too even though men may not have a distinct and full expectation of them. (6) Opportunities once neglected may never be recalled. (7) The consequences of folly and extravagance are often irretrievable. (8) Neglect is often attended with consequences as dreadful as positive misbehavior. (9) Many such consequences—as, *e. g.*, mortal diseases—are permanent and irretrievable to him who incurs them.

The character of the punishment, then, is analogous to that pronounced against transgressors by the Scriptures. Moreover, these things are not accidental, but they are things of every day's experience, and they proceed from general laws, and very general ones, by which God governs the world, in the natural course of his providence. This proves him to be an intelligent *Governor*, administering rewards and punishments. Moreover, he is a *moral* Governor; for though it is admitted that the divine government we are under in this present state, *taken alone*, and not with what we claim for the future administration of rewards and punishments, is not *perfect* in *degree*, it is yet *moral* in *kind*. For, not only is it to be presumed, since it is shown he does govern in some way, that he would govern agreeably to morality, but a moral government is implied also: (1) from the fact that human society, which is but an instrumentality of God, does actually punish the vicious; (2) from the fact that, in the natural course of things, virtue is rewarded and vice is punished. Therefore, the good and the bad effects, the satisfaction and the uneasiness produced, respectively, by virtue and by vice; the disposition of men to befriend virtue and to discountenance vice; lastly, the tendency that there is in virtue and vice to produce their good and bad effects in a greater degree than they do in fact produce them, owing to the imperfection of human society and human laws—all these are proofs of there being something moral in nature. For happy would be the lot of individuals and whole nations if perfect morality universally existed.

3. The foregoing considerations, therefore, are a strong proof, (1) that the Author of nature is in favor of virtue, and against vice; (2) that the distributive justice of the next world will be the very same in *kind*, however different in *degree*, from that which we now experience; (3) that virtue and vice, which are here actually rewarded and punished imperfectly, will be actually rewarded and punished fully hereafter. Finally, from all these con-

siderations there arises a presumption that the moral government established in nature will be carried on much farther hereafter, and indeed absolutely completed.

4. Our present life is a probation, under trial, difficulties, and danger, intended to prepare us, by moral discipline, for another world. The way to temporal good is a way of labor and trial, and beset with difficulty and danger, so that we are accustomed to feel anxious solicitude for the young just setting out in life. Persons may be betrayed into wrong behavior by surprise, or overcome by other very singular and extraordinary occasions. And again, persons who have contracted habits of vice and folly of any kind, are liable even to go out of the way to seek opportunities to gratify those habits. Some have so little consideration that they will scarce look beyond the present, but gratify themselves regardless of future consequences; some are blinded and deceived by inordinate passions, and some are not blinded, but forcibly carried away, as it were, by such passions; while some shamelessly avow that their pleasure is the law of their life, to whatever vicious excess it may carry them. Now, to secure worldly success, it is necessary to practice self-denial, and make the considerations of future interest govern the life, rather

than the enjoyments of the present. Thus we see that our difficulties and trials are of similar character, and have the same effect upon our behavior and future happiness, in things of merely worldly concern, as we are taught they have in religion. And, it may be added, in the former as well as in the latter, our dangers and difficulties are greatly increased by the ill-behavior of others, by improper education, by bad example, by wrong opinions being prevalent, and by the deceit and hypocrisy of those with whom we may be connected in business, etc. Nevertheless, in both it is possible for us to be prudent and careful: there is no more required of us than we are able to do; and, in any case, we can no more complain of this, with regard to the Author of nature, than of his not having given us other advantages belonging to other orders of creatures. All this, then, makes it credible that we are in a state of trial in our moral as well as in our natural capacity, notwithstanding these difficulties.

Farther, we are placed in this state of trial for our moral discipline—our improvement in virtue and piety—in preparation for another world. All the reasons for such a state existing here we may not be able to understand, but this is the *end* for which we are placed in such a state; so that just as the beginning of life is the time for education for mature age in this world, so is this life an education for the next world. 1. Our characters and qualifications must be suited to the particular kind of employments and happiness peculiar to the future world of bliss, for otherwise we should be incapable of engaging in those employments, and of enjoying that happiness. 2. We are so constituted that we are capable of becoming qualified for states of life for which we were once wholly unqualified. We can acquire habits of body and habits of mind. By accustoming ourselves to any course of action we get an aptness to go on, a facility, a readiness, and often pleasure, in it. The inclinations which rendered us averse to it grow weaker, the difficulties in it — not only the imaginary but the real ones—lessen, and the contrary principles grow stronger by exercise. And thus a new character, in several respects, may be formed. 3. These capacities are necessary to our preparation for mature life, and intended to be used in order to that preparation. Nature *in no respect* qualifies us at the beginning of life for this *mature* state of life, but leaves man an unformed, unfinished creature, utterly deficient, and unqualified, both in body and mind, for that mature state of life which was the end in view in his creation, considering him as related only to this world. All these defects are to be supplied by education through the capacities given him; and as nature has given us such capacities, so also she places us in such a situation throughout infancy, childhood, and youth, as is fitted for our acquiring those qualifications of all sorts of which we stand in need in mature age. In like manner the Scriptures represent this life as intended to educate us morally for the next. And this, though we could not see in what way it was so, for neither do children understand how food, exercise, etc., prepare them for mature age. But, 4. The present life is well fitted for this education. For, 1st. Virtue and piety are necessary qualifications for the future state, since, according to analogy, that state will be an active one, under a more immediate moral government by God, and thus give occasion for the need of such a character in its members. 2d. We need such improvement in our moral character by discipline. That we are capable of it, has been already shown; that we need it, is evident from our being, first, finite creatures, and therefore imperfect and deficient; secondly, corrupt creatures, and therefore needing renovation. Even unfallen creatures, as angels and Adam, are benefited by being raised to a higher and more secure state of virtue by proper discipline, while for fallen and depraved men it is absolutely necessary. Now, this world is *peculiarly fit* to be such a state of discipline to all who will set themselves to amendment and improvement. The existence about us of allurements to what is wrong, difficulties in the discharge of our duty, our not being able to act a uniform right part without some thought and care, the opportunities we have for doing wrong—these snares and temptations to vice compel us to keep upon our guard, and to practice resolution and self-denial in order to preserve our integrity. Thus a more continued and more intense exercise of virtue is required, and so the habit of virtue is better formed and fixed. And the same is true as to the formation of our habits of passive submission to God, necessary, together with that of active obedience, to make up an entirely virtuous character, such as is required for participation in the employments and the happiness of the next world. Affliction is the proper discipline for resignation. Just as we find, then, in this life, that what we *are to be* in mature age depends on what we *do* in childhood and youth, so we are to *be* in the next world just as we *do* here.

6. Such a system is not inconsistent with

wisdom and goodness. (1) It is quite credible that God's moral government is a scheme beyond our comprehension. The whole scheme of the material world and its government has such an astonishing connection of parts, such reciprocal correspondencies and mutual relations, that we do not know how necessary the existence of any one part, however small, may be to the existence of the whole; nor are we competent to judge of it as a whole. Much more incompetent are we to judge as to the moral world, from the small part which comes within our view, in the present life, of the true relations or importance of all its parts, or of its character as a whole. Therefore, we are not competent to say that it is inconsistent with wisdom or goodness. (2) Besides, we have no reason to infer, from the existence of evil, such a conclusion; for in the natural world no ends are accomplished without means, and often desirable ends are brought about by means which would otherwise be very undesirable. Supposing the moral world to be analogous to it in this respect, the afflictions we suffer may be the means by which a greater preponderance of good will, in the end, be secured. Farther, the natural government of the world is carried on by the operation of general laws, for which there may be the wisest reasons, and by which the best ends may be accomplished. There is no ground for believing that irregularities could be remedied or precluded by general laws, while special interpositions might produce evil, and prevent good, by encouraging idleness and negligence, and by making it doubtful what are the general and regular rules of life. So Christianity also is a scheme beyond our comprehension, itself but a part of a mysterious whole, viz., the moral government of the universe by God —a scheme in which means are used to an end —a scheme carried on by general laws.

Thus these analogies show us that it is not at all incredible that, could we but comprehend the whole, we should find the permission of disorder in the world consistent with justice and goodness. Therefore, the fact of its existence cannot invalidate the proof that we have of religion. We are only incompetent to judge in such cases when we are ignorant of the possibilities of things, and of their present relations; and we dare not venture to declare that the existence of evil is inconsistent with infinite wisdom, and goodness, and power.

7. We must expect that such a system will have some things in it incomprehensible to us. (1) There are innumerable things in the constitution and government of the universe

which are beyond the natural reach of our faculties. Those that are open to our view are doubtless but a point in comparison with the whole plan of Providence as to things past as well as future in this world, not to speak of what is now going on also in the remote parts of the boundless universe. And even those things we do see are, in many respects, beyond our powers of comprehension. But this is no presumption against their truth and reality; and therefore there is no presumption either against the truth of Christianity because it teaches us some truths which are incomprehensible to us—as, *e. g.*, the government of the world by Jesus Christ, the influence of the Holy Spirit upon the hearts of men, etc.

(2) Since the acknowledged constitution and course of nature is not what we should expect beforehand, but apparently in many respects objectionable, and since we thus know that we are wholly incompetent to judge of such matters beforehand, we must conclude that we are also incompetent, only in a much higher degree, to judge beforehand what Christianity ought to be. How improbable, *e. g.*, it would have seemed beforehand that men should be so much more capable of discovering the general laws of matter, and the magnitudes,

paths, and revolutions of the heavenly bodies, than the causes and cures of diseases, and many other things in which human life seems so much more nearly concerned than astronomy; or how improbable that brutes, without reason, should act through instinct, in many respects with vastly greater sagacity and foresight than men. Yet such are the facts, and the short-sightedness of our reason, even in the commoner matters of this life, is thus fully seen.

(3) Farther still, there is a great resemblance between the light of nature and the light of Christianity in this respect. In both, (1) the common rules of conduct are plain and obvious; (2) many parts of knowledge require careful consideration to gain it; (3) the hinderances—viz., indolence, self-satisfaction, our love of other things, and the weakness of our minds, etc.—are the same in both; (4) they are to be increased in the same way, by the continuance of liberty and the progress of learning; and (5) we should expect that Christianity, being a remedial system, would have been long delayed, and at last but partially and imperfectly communicated to mankind as a whole. For many of the remedies that we possess for physical diseases were unknown for ages, are now known to but few, and probably many are yet entirely unknown.

We conclude, then, that reason is incompetent to decide against revelation because of any thing in its moral teachings, as also to reject its evidences because of the difficulty of comprehending some of its teachings. Neither can Christianity be rejected because it is a complicated scheme, involving a long series of intricate means to accomplish the recovery of the world from sin, for such is the natural course of providence in this world. Throughout nature its Author appears deliberate in his operations, accomplishing his ends by slow, successive steps—as, for instance, in the changes of the seasons, the ripening of the fruits of the earth, etc.

8. We should expect the appointment of a Mediator between God and man, in the work of human redemption, by whom the redemption of the world would be accomplished. (1) We, and all reasonable creatures, are indebted for life and all life's blessings, first, for our being brought into the world, and then for our preservation and happiness therein to the mediation and instrumentality of others. (2) It is supposable that future punishment may follow wickedness as a natural consequence, according to general laws established in the universe, just as evil consequences follow our transgressions in this world. (3) But we find

that, in the constitution of nature, all the usual bad consequences of evil actions do not always follow, but that sometimes, in various degrees, they may be prevented, so that we have here some evidence of compassion in the original constitution of the world. (4) There seems no reason to suppose that any thing *we* could do would, *of itself*, prevent them, for we do not know all the reasons why future punishment should be inflicted, nor the whole consequences of vice, nor the manner in which they would follow if unprevented. The analogy of nature gives us positive evidence that when men, by their folly, bring on themselves temporal injury, disease, and ruin, neither sorrow for the past, nor amendment for the future, will prevent these consequences. Therefore, if we misbehave in our higher capacity, we should not expect that sorrow and amendment would alone be sufficient to prevent our punishment. (5) That we are in a state of degradation and danger, through the fault of our first parents, is analogous to the whole history of man here, as when we see children, for instance, daily brought into a worse state in the world through the misbehavior of their parents. Being therefore in such a fallen state, and being guilty ourselves of many actual sins besides, and having no way of escape, the Scriptures assure us

8*

that God gave his Son to the world, that whosoever would believe on him should not perish, and that his interposition to that end was effectual. (6) In this revelation we should expect to find much, the reason of which we cannot know. For instance, it tells us the way in which Christ so interposed for us—1st. As a Prophet, to publish anew the law of God; 2d. As a King, to found the Church, and to govern it by his Spirit; 3d. As a Priest, to offer himself a propitiatory sacrifice, and make atonement for the sins of the world. Now, without a revelation we should have no means of knowing whether or not a Mediator was necessary; or, supposing one to be necessary, in what manner he would effect the object for which he had come. It is therefore highly absurd to object to the expediency, or usefulness, for instance, of the sacrificial death of Christ for our redemption, because we may not see how it was conducive to the ends proposed. (7) Such a revelation of the Innocent One suffering for the guilty is consistent with the analogy of nature; for in this life innocent people ordinarily suffer for the faults of the guilty; and it is often the case, when men, by their follies and crimes, have been brought into extreme distress, from which they can be extricated only by the very great pains and labors of others, that the guilty are saved through the sufferings of the innocent. Besides, the tendency of this method of our redemption is to vindicate the authority of God's laws, and to deter his creatures from sin in the most effectual manner; and this consideration alone is sufficient to justify its reasonableness. Yet this is probably far from being the whole reason. There may be many reasons of which we know nothing; nor is our ignorance of the reasons a good ground for denying its reasonableness. On the contrary, the analogy of nature teaches us not to expect so much to know the reasons of the divine conduct as to be informed of our duty; for we know but little about the fundamental principles of the operations of nature, yet we are sufficiently informed as to the practical effect of those operations upon our lives. So with revelation. The doctrine of a Mediator relates only to what was done on God's part in the appointment of a Mediator, and on the Mediator's part in the execution of the work thus assigned him. Our duty in regard to that mediation is entirely a different matter. On this we *are* fully informed; we need not be so informed upon the other.

9. We ought not to expect that Christianity should be clearly proved, or universally believed. For—1st. It is often exceedingly

difficult to determine wherein our *temporal* interests consist, or to estimate the changes and accidents which may disappoint our plans, or to answer objections to a course of action, which, nevertheless, for good reasons, we feel warranted in pursuing. 2d. The blessings of this life—of climate, soil, health, strength, understanding, and knowledge—are distributed among men in the most unequal and promiscuous manner. 3d. Nor are these facts inconsistent with justice, since no more is required of any man than what might equitably be expected of him. Nor is it inconsistent with wisdom and goodness; for (1) the examination of the evidence of religion, to those to whom it does not appear convincing at first, may be part of their trial, in giving scope for a virtuous exercise or a vicious neglect of their understanding, in examining or not examining it, just as they are in a state of probation as to their behavior in other and more common affairs. The same disposition which makes a man obedient to the precepts of religion would lead him, were he not convinced of its truth, to consider its evidence. Negligence and inattention, before conviction, are as truly guilty as vicious practice afterward. (2) Even doubtful evidence places us in a state of probation in so far as that we are bound to consider and weigh that evidence. Doubt implies some evidence of that which is doubted, just as truly as belief implies a higher degree of it, and certainty a higher degree still. Therefore, even doubt requires of us a reverent and careful consideration, that is open to farther light and conviction. (3) Difficulties of belief should no more be complained of than difficulties of practice; for, since they give occasion for the exercise of a virtuous disposition, they are of the same nature as external temptation, and are adapted for our discipline and improvement in virtue.

In conclusion, let us consider: 1st. That these difficulties may be from our own fault—from our attending less to evidence than to difficulties, or from considering religion with levity or carelessness, with passion or with prejudice. These may hinder evidence from being laid before us, or prevent it from being candidly weighed after it has been presented. 2d. That therefore, if some will continue to disregard and reject Christianity, without a candid consideration of its evidences, there is no reason to suppose that they would act otherwise, even though a demonstration of its truth were given them. 3d. That the guilt of an immoral life in those who thus obstinately reject the light of Christianity, without a fair examination of its evidences, is greatly aggravated.

Such is the argument drawn from the agreement of Christianity with the acknowledged constitution and course of nature. Nothing appears contrary to nature, and there is much that is in complete and remarkable harmony therewith. This fact points to the Maker of nature as the Author of Christianity also; and, while its singular analogy with the order of nature about us attests its reality and truth, the impress of the same great features and principles of administration upon both declares that both are the work of the same infinite Power and Wisdom, and that the Author of Christianity also is God.

III. But Christianity excels alike the best deductions of philosophy and the highest teachings of nature. While it is in agreement with them, it is also superior, and thus it displays its divinity. This has already been partially shown (*vide* Part I., Ch. 3), and we have seen how Christ alone has, 1st, set forth the whole vast range of moral truth; 2d, has taught with unvarying wisdom and goodness. In these and other such striking characteristics is his superiority to all other teachers shown. In the nature of the *special* characteristics of his teaching this is more apparent still. Rogers

("Supernatural Origin of the Bible") has pointed out, among other peculiarities distinguishing the teaching contained in the Bible from that of all other religions and philosophies, deprived of its light, the following particulars: 1. The propounding of a religion which aspires to universal dominion, and that achieved without violence, by moral suasion alone, notwithstanding that that religion is contrary to our fallen nature, and often violated even by its own professed followers. 2. The full recognition of the right of conscience in general, and of the principle of universal toleration, found nowhere else, especially never with a *Jew*. 3. In broad contrast with all other systems, its giving no hint of any alliance between religion and political government. 4. Similarly, its reticence as to the future and invisible world, excepting on the one point as to which they are silent—viz., that therein "dwelleth righteousness." 5. Its teaching of the *entire* helplessness of man for good—exemplified in Christ's assertion, "Without me ye can do nothing"—while yet it remains most sympathetic with man's sad condition. 6. Its principle, that to conscientiously reduce to practice what we already know ("He that is disposed to do the will of God shall know of the doctrine"), is the surest way of advancing in the knowledge of divine truth. 7. That no religious knowledge is of any worth except as reduced to practice—"faith without works is dead." 8. Its freedom from minute casuistry—as, *e. g.*, in the case of "meats," "days," etc. 9. Its giving the crowning place to "charity." 10. Its avoidance of political and social rocks—as the questions of slavery and those pertaining to civil government. In all these it is in the strongest contrast not only with all philosophy, but with human nature generally, and even with the opinions and practices, in one point or another, of most of its followers in succeeding times; for they, after having been taught, still vainly strove to reach, in their own instructions, the height of Christ's divine teaching.

Row also sets forth Christ's superiority, substantially as follows:

1. Christ's declaration, "I am the light of the world; he that followeth me shall not walk in darkness, but shall have the light of life," was a great and bold utterance in view of the coming tests of the ages of time, but completely verified on every page of history since, and by the world to-day. But if so, he far transcends in this all philosophers, or other teachers, that have ever appeared among men, and therefore he must be superhuman and divine.

2. No human genius, however exalted, has ever been able wholly to emancipate himself from the restraints imposed on him by his birth, and by the moral and spiritual atmosphere in which he was educated. For instance, the teachings of Mohammed, in the Koran, bear the strongest impress of the Arab mind, as also that of all others who have assumed to be the great moral teachers of mankind. They have always been in some degree national, or local. Jesus Christ alone is catholic as humanity. Yet the Jews of his time were proverbially narrow-minded and exclusive bigots, fanatical and superstitious, and in such an atmosphere must Jesus and his disciples have been born and educated. It is evident that in that atmosphere the highest moral teaching could not have been evolved by any natural process; consequently, if Jewish peasants and fishermen have succeeded in elaborating a body of doctrine which not only agrees, so far as it goes, with that of the most enlightened teachers of the ancient world, but also succeeded in accomplishing what all of those masters, after all their efforts, failed utterly to effect, the conclusion, upon every reasonable principle, must be that Christ, the first Promulgator of this doctrine, was more than man.

3. The teaching of Christ is far superior to that of the philosophers, as well as to the teachings of mere nature: 1st. In its intense earnestness and reality, and in its appeal to every principle—the love of God, the love of Christ, the feeling of benevolence, self-love, the perception of moral beauty, the sense of truth, the love of justice, the appreciation of the honorable, the sense of self-respect, the love of approbation, and even the desire for praise—to all, in short, that acts mightily on human nature. This is in the most striking contrast with the philosophers, both ancient and modern. A large part of their attention is directed to mere abstract speculation—as, *e. g.*, concerning the grounds and nature of moral obligation, in which, as they have determined in favor of one or the other theory, they have elaborated systems based on partial principles, and in disregard of some of the great realities of man's moral constitution, besides being otherwise partial and local. But the New Testament is catholic as human nature. 2d. In its entire freedom from all attempts to deal with either political or social questions, and that too when Christ professed to be the Founder of a kingdom. The universal practice of the great philosophers of the ancient world (cf. Ueberweg's "History of Phi-

losophy") was precisely the reverse. With them, in fact, ethics was but a branch of politics. The political and social legislation in the religion of Mohammed, also, is well known as the rock on which it is being hopelessly shipwrecked. Against Christianity, on the other hand, it has been charged as a defect in its principles, that it dwells so little on public duties and virtues; but it is evident that in this it is singularly wise. If Christ had thus begun his work of regenerating mankind, Christianity would not have survived the century which gave it birth. In its avoidance, then, of this danger we see the evidence of superior wisdom, and realize that its Author must have possessed an insight more than human. 3d. It has founded the religion of humanity. "Ye shall neither in this mountain, nor yet at Jerusalem, worship the Father; . . . but the hour cometh, and now is, when the true worshipers shall worship the Father in spirit and in truth; for the Father seeketh such to worship him. God is a Spirit; and they that worship him must worship him in spirit and in truth," said Jesus to the Samaritan woman (John iv. 20–24). In thus repudiating at once all that was national, local, and outward, Jesus founded his religion, his spirituality, and the spirituality of true worship. Even Renan says that in this utterance he has "forever laid deep the foundation of the religion of universal humanity." 4th. Its all-comprehensive law of duty, declaring man's duty to man: (1) As founded on, and originating in, his filial relation to God as the universal Father of all men, and giving rise thereby to the universal brotherhood of man. The latter principle was but dimly conceived, at best, by any of the ancients, and then only as a barren speculation; while also all modern anti-Christian systems find it impossible to announce any principle (cf., *e. g.*, that men are the descendants of some primeval savage, or that we should practice self-sacrifice for others, because it is, on the whole, more *expedient*, etc.) which can form any effectual basis upon which it may rest. (2) As measured by the regard which man feels for himself—"Do unto others as ye would have them do unto you," etc. (3) As measured and sanctioned by the obligation he is under to Jesus Christ. "Love one another as I have loved you," he bids us—carrying the law of duty and self-sacrifice to its extremest limits, beyond which it is impossible for human thought to pass, and including every social duty which man can owe to man. 5th. That every mental gift, worldly possession, or other advantage, which man possesses, as well as the position in society he occupies, is a stewardship intrusted to him by God, for the right discharge of which he is responsible. 6th. The relative importance he assigns to the milder virtues—as meekness, pity, and especially humility (*vide* Sermon on the Mount), making them predominant, while the philosophers have ever put highest the political or heroic virtues of courage, patriotism, and ambition. But ever *since* Christ, it cannot be doubted that an overwhelming majority of the wisest and holiest of men have accepted this teaching as right; and it is evident that if those principles had, during the last three thousand years, occupied the place of the heroic virtues in men's estimation, the happiness of mankind would have increased a thousandfold. 7th. Christ viewed his mission as to the masses of mankind; the philosophers and the followers of natural religion, to a small intellectual aristocracy, and "to those of mankind who have a natural tendency to virtue," as Plato said—while Christ came not to "call the righteous, but sinners, to repentance." 8th. The creation by Christianity of a mighty moral and spiritual power adequate to effect the regeneration of mankind. Of the want of this the ancient philosophers confessed their need, but never even claimed they had wherewith to heal the acknowledged moral corruption of man (*vide* Aristotle, "Ethics," book x., ch. 10). They never even thought of preaching repentance and amendment to the masses of men, and only a small body of ingenuous youths, born with a natural tendency toward what is good and noble, were supposed capable of receiving their instructions. They could only appeal to the love of the beautiful and the good, or to the powerful principle of habit, and such like springs of action. But what were these to those who, without any new principle of moral life, or powerful conviction, were already vicious, and already under the dominion of bad habits? All that could be done for such persons was to bring upon them the external power of coercion. Hence the political character of all the ancient, and several of the modern, systems of ethics.* (Also cf. the doc-

---

* Consider also the full significance of the following testimonies: "The farther the ages advance in cultivation, the more can the Bible be used, partly as the foundation, partly as the means, of education—not, of course, by superficial, but by really wise, men."—*Goethe.* "I have examined all, as well as my narrow sphere, my straitened means, and my busy life, would allow me, and the result is, the Bible is the best book in the world."—*J. Adams.* "Peruse the books of philosophers, with all their pomp and diction—how meager, how contemptible, are they when compared with the Scriptures! The majesty of the Scriptures strikes me with admiration."—*Rousseau.* "I have always been strongly in favor of secular education—in the sense of edu-

trine of "the survival of the fittest"—the ministration of death to the *degraded* masses of mankind.)

But Christ created a moral and spiritual power capable of stirring the hearts of men to their lowest depths—*i. e.*, faith, which, if we grant to the skeptic, for the sake of argument, that such changes are not the product of supernatural power working directly upon the soul, has actually succeeded in recovering to holiness a multitude of fallen men, such as no man can number. He has likewise created the greatest of Societies—namely, the Christian Church—in which the subjects of his spiritual kingdom may be trained to holiness; for faith produces a conviction in the innermost spirit of

---

cation without theology—but I must confess I have been no less seriously perplexed to know by what practical measures the religious feeling, which is the essential basis of conduct, was to be kept up, in the present utterly chaotic state of opinion on these matters, without the use of the Bible. The pagan moralists lack life and color, and even the noble Stoic, Marcus Antoninus, is too high and refined for an ordinary child. Take the Bible as a whole, make the severest deductions which fair criticism can dictate, and there still remains in this old literature a vast residuum of moral beauty and grandeur. By the study of what other book could children be so much humanized? If Bible-reading is not accompanied by constraint and solemnity, I do not believe there is any thing in which children take more pleasure."—*Huxley.*

man, respecting the eternal realities of things, and thus concentrates on the conscience the whole force of the religious principle in man. It then presents to him the person of Jesus in the divine attractiveness of his life and death—the perfect embodiment of all that is pure, holy, and lovely, in God or man, as the center of a new spiritual life; and thus has it restored to holiness multitudes of degraded men, and has elevated every holy man who has come under its influence to yet higher degrees of holiness. But neither philosophy nor the system of natural religion has had any very profound convictions; it professed even to deal only in probabilities. The philosopher, therefore, could not grapple with the conscience. All he could do was to appeal to cold reason; he could awaken no emotion, nor summon any force capable of overcoming the violence of the passions. The best he could do was to form an ideal republic, or a shadowy, abstract system of morals—while Christ has created the Christian Church.

Thus does Christianity show its superiority to all that has originated from merely human deduction, or is taught by the light of nature alone. In its original and unimprovable excellence; in its undisguised openness to all the world; in its adaptation to every state, disposition, and capacity, of man; in its spirituality of worship, its humbling of men, and its exaltation of the Deity; in its restoration of order to the world; its tendency to eradicate all evil passions from the heart; its contrariety to the covetousness and ambition of mankind; its restoration of the divine image to man, instead, as other religions, of weakly and viciously affixing the moral image of man on God, and in its mighty effects—in all alike, Christianity is far superior to aught else that has ever appeared in the world, and in its greatness and glory proclaims itself as no less than divine.

We next proceed to consider the prophecies of Christ.

CHAPTER V.

THE EVIDENCE OF PROPHECY.

Prophecies, as we have seen, are "miracles of knowledge," and, consisting in "the declaration of things future beyond the power of human sagacity to discern or calculate, they are the highest evidence that can be given of a revelation from God." Christianity, bearing not one only but all the marks of divinity that we can require, and challenging from every side the closest inspection of her claims, invites us to behold also this "highest evidence" of prophecy, and to see that in all her aspects there is displayed the glory of her divine origin. In bringing this class of evidences forward, we are entitled to cite the prophecies contained in the Old Testament, as well as those in the New, in support of our position; for it is evident to every candid mind that, whether divine or not, all contained in both divisions of the Bible forms but one great system in successive phases of development, from the patriarchs to Christ. Whatsoever, therefore, goes to prove the divinity of any stage of that development, is evidence of the divinity of the organic whole, and of every other stage. If Judaism was divine, then must Christianity also—which is but the perfected fruit of Judaism divested at length of its old, hardened, and burst shell of ritualism—be divine. Moreover, many of the most explicit of the Old Testament prophecies relate directly and plainly to Christianity, and testify expressly to its divine origin. From the nature of the case, too, the argument derived from the fulfillment of the prophecies contained in the Old Testament is far fuller than that from the fulfillment of those in the New. The simple fact that the latter were delivered so much later than the former, necessarily causes their fulfillment to be as yet more incomplete. The larger part of the latter probably still remain to be fulfilled, but most of the former have already completely come to pass. The argument, therefore, drawn from the prophecies of the New Testament, is as yet much more limited than if it were extended also to those of the Old. Nevertheless, we will confine ourselves entirely to those delivered by our Lord — merely asking the reader to bear in mind also those already cited from the Old Testament—feeling confident that a sufficient number even of these will be found to be true beyond all reasonable doubt. Keeping in mind, then, how much the argument is strengthened by the accomplished fulfillment of the older prophecies, and reflecting that therefore it is not unreasonable to expect it to continually gather fresh force from the future accomplishment of most of the later, we cite the following plain predictions of Christ, of whose fulfillment no one can doubt:

1. Christ distinctly foretold his death and its circumstances. In Matthew it is said: "From that time forth [or about a year and a half before his crucifixion; cf. Lange on Matt. vi. 13-21; ii. 6, etc.] began Jesus to show unto his disciples how that he must go unto Jerusalem, and suffer many things of the elders, and chief priests, and scribes, and be killed, and be raised again the third day" (Matt. xvi. 21). Mark says: "And he began to teach them that the Son of man must suffer many things, and be rejected of the elders, and of the chief priests, and scribes, and be killed, and after three days rise again" (Mark viii. 31). Luke, that he said: "The Son of man must suffer many things, and be rejected of the elders, and chief priests, and scribes, and be slain, and be raised the third day" (Luke ix. 22). Here are three separate and independent testimonies to the fact that he uttered a prediction of his sufferings in general, of his rejection by the chief priests and scribes, that he should die a

violent death, and that on the third day he should rise again. We have seen how impossible (Part I., Ch. 4) it is that the accounts of the Gospel were forged. The differences which otherwise exist between their different authors, prove that they were not in collusion. Their substantial agreement, therefore, on the other hand, shows that their accounts are true. And the minute mention of the various circumstances above, of the sufferings, rejection, death, and resurrection, predicted of Christ by himself, is a strong mark of his divine mission. Moreover, he also predicted (Matt. xx. 18, 19) that he "should be betrayed;" that the *scribes* should "*condemn* him to death;" that *they* should "deliver him to the Gentiles;" that they should do this for the *Gentiles* (1) "to mock;" (2) "to scourge;" and (3) "to *crucify* him;" and afterward (Matt. xxvi. 23–25), that it should be Judas who should betray him; and still farther (Mark x. 33, 34), that the *Gentiles* should "*spit* upon him." Now, all these were precisely fulfilled. But no merely human foresight could have foretold such incidental circumstances. An enthusiast would not have anticipated his rejection and crucifixion at all, and an impostor would never have dared to give, beforehand, so numerous and so minute tests of the validity of his claims. The conclusion must be that Christ was a Prophet sent from God, and commissioned for a divine purpose.

2. This is still more strongly the case with his predictions of his resurrection. We have seen in the passages already quoted how distinctly he foretold it. It will be our task hereafter to show how certainly he did rise again on the third day. For the present, it will be sufficient to direct attention to the irresistible force of the evidence the fulfillment of this prophecy gives to the divinity of the mission of Christ; for however a man might venture to utter predictions as to his death and its circumstances, and through a wonderful but still human prescience be able to forecast them, minutely and correctly, yet never could a mere man foresee that he should be raised again from the dead, and that too on the third day. Yet Christ did so predict it: we think it will be made evident that thus it accordingly came to pass; and, putting aside for the present the evidence given in the miraculous nature of the occurrence itself, its prediction alone strongly proves the divine mission of him who uttered it.

3. We proceed to point out briefly some others of his prophecies fulfilled in later times. Such was that of the destruction of Jerusalem, with its attendant circumstances. Christ pre-

dicted (Luke xxi. 20-24), "When ye shall see Jerusalem compassed with armies, then know that the desolation thereof is nigh; . . . and they shall fall by the edge of the sword, and shall be led away captive into all nations;" that, speaking of Jerusalem (Luke xix. 43), "The days shall come upon thee that thine enemies shall cast a trench round about thee, and compass thee round, and keep thee in on every side;" and that, in respect to the temple (Matt. xxiv. 2), "The days will come, in the which there shall not be left here one stone upon another that shall not be thrown down." All this came exactly to pass. Beyond all question (cf. Part I., Ch. 4), the accounts contained in the Gospels were in existence before that time. No scholar, however skeptical, will deny this. Yet it is a notorious historical fact (*vide* Josephus, De Bello. Jud. Lib. i.-vi.) that Jerusalem, about forty years afterward, was thus besieged by Titus, a trench was literally cast around it, and it was entirely surrounded by the Roman armies; so that it was really "compassed round, and kept in on every side." Moreover, when taken, it was completely "desolated," its inhabitants "fell by the sword, and were led away captive into all nations," being sold by thousands as slaves into the surrounding nations, and the temple was utterly and remarkably destroyed, so that there was not "left one stone upon another that was not cast down."

4. Still more remarkable is his prediction of the continued subjugation of Jerusalem following its capture. In the same passage of Luke (xxi. 24) he said, "And Jerusalem shall be *trodden down* of the Gentiles until the times of the Gentiles be fulfilled." In this prophecy, following in immediate connection that of the capture and devastation of Jerusalem, it is implied (1) that, from the time of this capture, Jerusalem, for a long, indefinite time, should continue to exist as a city—"trodden down," not destroyed; (2) that its condition during that time should be not that of freedom, but of subjugation, by "the Gentiles," and that of the most grievous and humiliating kind— "*trodden down;*" (3) and, finally, it is intimated that at last, when "the times of the Gentiles" should have been fulfilled, it shall be no longer "trodden down of the Gentiles." Every one of these particulars, except the last, predicted, beyond all cavil, at least eighteen hundred years ago, has been already signally fulfilled. (1) Jerusalem has never ceased to exist as a city. While Babylon and Tyre, Corinth, Ephesus, and many others, that were overwhelmed by the fire and sword of the Ro-

man, or sunk under the still surer ravages of time, have risen no more, Jerusalem has ever remained an inhabited city. Who but Omniscience, that could have even foreseen her terrible devastations, could have also anticipated her recovery? (2) Nevertheless, it has also ever since continued to this day in abject subjugation to "the Gentiles." After the Romans, the Persians succeeded to the dominion over it; from them the Mohammedan invaders of Arabia wrested it; then the Crusaders; again the Arabians, and lastly the Turks, have successively occupied it unto this day. Moreover, the condition of the Jews in their own holy city has been more constantly miserable than perhaps anywhere else in the world. Even now they are treated with greater cruelty and contempt in Jerusalem, by its Turkish conquerors, than are the people of any other nation, strangers or natives. In A.D. 135 the Romans, after suppressing a revolt made by the Jews, forbade them, on pain of death, from even entering the city, and that prohibition lasted till the time of Constantine, A.D. 300–337, when it was repealed, but only so far as that they were allowed to enter it once a year, to wail over the desolation of "the holy and beautiful house in which their fathers worshiped God" (*vide* McClintock and Strong's Cyclopædia, Art. Jerusalem); and ever since, the Jews have there been under peculiar oppression. Thus Christ's words have been, through eighteen hundred years, precisely fulfilled, and Jerusalem has been "trodden down of the Gentiles." (3) From the expression used, that thus it should be *"until the times of the Gentiles be fulfilled,"* it is probably a correct inference to draw that when those "times" shall have been accomplished, Jerusalem shall be no more trodden down, and the Jew no longer a reproach in the earth, but both shall resume that independence, prosperity, and greatness of station among the nations, which they had before. This, of course, still remains unfulfilled; but the remarkable fact of the preservation of the Jews as a nation, through the ages, though "scattered" among all nations, and "peeled," if it does not directly point to its accomplishment, at least proves its possibility; while for the first time in so many centuries it has of late at last seemed capable of being fulfilled, and we have been hearing from time to time of the probability, under the influence of recent great political changes, etc., of the Jew once more resuming his dominion of the land and city of his fathers.

5. Christ prophesied also (Matt. xxiv. 14) that "this gospel of the kingdom shall be

preached in all the world for a witness unto all nations." Nothing seemed then more unlikely to human foresight than this. Judea itself was but a small and despised country, and the Jews were everywhere held in detestation. How unlikely that a doctrine originating among Jews, and preached by Jews, without either the learning of the Greek or the power of the Roman to recommend it, should yet find its way down the remotest ages of posterity, and throughout all nations! For Christ's doctrine was rejected *even by the leaders of the Jewish nation itself*, and he executed by them, and his followers persecuted, as also they afterward were by the whole power of the Roman Government, in ten great successive persecutions. How improbable did it seem that it could at all survive, when its own nation had disowned it, and was striving to stamp it out of existence! or, if it might linger obscurely among the hills and valleys of Galilee, how unlikely for it to ever spread abroad, even to the neighboring and kindred tribes! and how utterly impossible that it should ever prevail in distant continents, and among strange and unknown races of men! *And what impostor would have dared to give by such a declaration such a test for succeeding ages, by which they might so easily expose and ridicule his claims?* Yet, standing where we are to-day, we behold the preaching of the gospel fast extending to every land under heaven. Almost already is the prophecy fulfilled. The next generation will, without doubt, behold every nation and tribe, even to the smallest and most obscure, visited by the missionary of the gospel of Jesus Christ.

6. Christ also predicted that he should have an enduring Church. He said (Matt. xvi. 18), "Upon this rock I will build my Church, and the gates of hell shall not prevail against it." This too seemed most improbable. When, rejected by the Jews themselves, despised by the wisdom-loving Greeks, and persecuted unrelentingly by the all-powerful Romans; when all of earth that was esteemed wise and powerful was to unite in contemning and extirpating it—it was a bold prophecy to foretell, nevertheless, its perpetual existence. When the walls of Babylon and Tyre, and the world-wide empire of Alexander, had already fallen into the dust before their various enemies, and the great empires of Persia, Rome, and of the Saracens, were destined to fall in their turn, it was most improbable that that of the Peasant of Galilee should continue, victorious over all the "gates of hell," to remotest times, and in remotest nations. Nevertheless, so it has re-

ally been. Christ's Church is stronger to-day than ever before.

We confidently offer, then, these prophecies as infallible marks of the divine mission of Christ, and therefore of the divinity of Christianity — the result of that mission. They prove him to have been supernaturally endowed with a knowledge of the future, such as has never been approached, in the slightest degree, by any one, however wise, outside of the prophets of the Bible. The predictions alleged of the ancient oracles are not worthy of comparison with them. Horne has shown in his "Introduction" that, in contrast with the prophecies of the Bible, those of the oracles—1. Gave no prediction spontaneously, but only when applied to, and paid for it. 2. Their obvious end was to satisfy some trivial curiosity, or to aid some ambitious man in his designs. 3. They were never given except after elaborate, prescribed ceremonies, the neglect or wrong observance of any one of which was said to vitiate the whole proceeding—thus giving an easy way of accounting for a failure in the accomplishment of the thing predicted. 4. The few oracles they at last gave related merely to some single, disconnected event. 5. They seldom or ever were of such a nature as to be in support of morality, purity, justice, etc. 6. They were generally ambiguous, and capable of being interpreted either way, according to the event. Thus the famous response rendered to Crœsus, when he was about to make war against the Persians, and had inquired whether he should succeed. The oracle declared that "he would destroy a great empire," which Crœsus interpreted to mean that he would destroy the Persians. But after having been ruined in the war himself, the oracle interpreted it to mean, that "he should destroy his own empire." 7. Their oracles did not extend beyond their own territories, nor more than a very few years into the future. 8. They were not committed to writing in books open to public inspection, so that their truth or falsity might afterward be examined. 9. Nevertheless, notwithstanding all the above means of escape from detection, the heathen oracles were frequently found to be unquestionably false, and, especially in later times, came to be held in utter contempt. On the contrary, the prophecies of Christ—1. Were delivered openly. 2. They were not such as flattered the national vanity, but such as humiliated the Jews, and with the accompaniment of the most fearful denunciations against them for their sins. 3. He gained no riches or power thereby, but persecution and death. 4.

His prophecies were a part of one great whole of prophecy, extending in a connected chain from Moses, and before Moses, down, and treating as its great subject-matter of the establishment and prosperity of the kingdom of Christ among men. 5. They are all in support of morality and true religion. 6. They are express and distinct, in many instances, as to the circumstances of the event predicted. 7. Usually they seemed most improbable at the time they were uttered. 8. They reached, in some cases, hundreds, and even thousands, of years forward, and embraced all nations in its view. 9. They were committed to writing, and have always been open to public inspection. 10. Not one has ever been shown to be false, while history, as it has during successive revolutions unfolded its changing pages, has proclaimed, one by one, at long intervals, the accomplishment of many of them.

Say what we may, human penetration is unequal to this. No man, however skillful and experienced, can, of his own powers, so forecast the coming future, or ever has predicted, or shall predict with perfect accuracy, a future state of things, involving a long, complicated, and connected series of events, extending over hundreds of years yet to come. Yet such are the prophecies of Christ. We confidently claim that they therefore bear the unmistakable impress of Him who " seeth all things from the beginning;" and standing, as they do, utterly without a parallel in the records of the human race, they prove that they, and the Christian system to which they bear witness, are superhuman and divine.

CHAPTER VI.

THE EVIDENCE OF MIRACLES—I. IN GENERAL.

To all the preceding we now add the evidence of miracles, both as affording its separate testimony, and as confirming the testimony of all that has gone before. It is, perhaps, impossible to define a miracle with any certainty, farther than by describing its visible results apparent in the person or thing upon which it has been wrought. To go farther, and attempt to define the process and means by which it has been accomplished, is surely always uncertain, and often likely to be positively false. That which is in its essential nature above the human cannot, it would seem, with any certainty, be discovered and known by powers that are themselves only human. Revelation may disclose it; but till revelation does disclose it, all our attempts are but more or less uncertain speculations. They may indeed happen to be true speculations, but it appears impossible for us to know certainly whether they are true or false till it be revealed to us by a superior Intelligence from on high. At any rate, since revelation has not told us how a miracle is wrought, we shall not attempt to explain it here. It will be sufficient to say, that by miracles we mean those great works which are commonly known by that name, related in the Bible as wrought by those who claimed to be commissioned from God to deliver his message to men. These we claim show superhuman wisdom and power attendant upon those who wrought them, and prove, whatever may have been the *modus operandi* of their performance, that those persons were indeed the authorized exponents of a divine message to men. It is no objection to this conclusion that we know not by what method this result has been accomplished. We may see the marks of divine power and wisdom in the result before us without knowing at all by what process it was done. We perceive, for example, these signs in the work of creation around us, yet we know nothing at all how God worked in accomplishing creation; we know only that in some way he has put forth his all-wise and all-powerful hand, and performed the work. In miracles, also, we may see the manifest tokens of the same omnipotent and omniscient Power, and in the same way, without knowing the process of his working, we may yet surely know and confess his presence. Nay, even in the accomplished works of man's power and skill—as a watch, a steam-engine, etc.—we may see in the results before us manifest evidence that there is a work that is certainly the product of an intelligence no less than human; we know that no brute, however sagacious, could have produced it; and yet we may not have the most distant conception of the *process* by which it has been made—how the metals were wrought from the ore, the parts made and adapted to each other, etc. And so with a miracle, wrought by the power of God attendant upon his messengers, or exercised by himself in the person of his Son—we may be convinced beyond a doubt that here there is "the finger of God," though we know nothing as to the manner in which God has wrought. It is, then, not necessary for us to enter into any explanation of the mode by which miracles have been wrought; it is sufficient for us to show that the miracles of Christ possess characteristics that are superhuman, and which show that Christianity therefore is divine.

1. First, let us notice in what manner miracles give evidence that Christianity is divine. 1st. They are in entire harmony with all the other superhuman characteristics of revelation. As we have seen, revelation, if given at all, must necessarily be miraculous. It is reasonable to expect, moreover, that the miraculous

should appear not only in the bare utterance of the revelation; for being uttered, as it is, by, or under the authority of, a divine power, present and exerted in the act of such utterance, we might reasonably expect that that miraculous power should also appear in the attendant circumstances, and such changes occur in the natural world around as in the ordinary course of things are unknown, and such as give visible evidence of the presence and active working of that power. Especially if it is a divine personage himself that speaks, would we expect not only that there should come from him divine truth, but also that there should break from him divine power, exerted in great and significant works of superhuman might, wisdom, and goodness. He who was of divine descent and divine character, whose teaching was above that of men, and who uttered such wondrous prophecies, we might well expect would also work miracles. The absence, then, of miracles would be a serious defect in the full and rounded completeness of the Christian Evidences. Their presence, therefore, harmonizes with the whole system, and adds an additional characteristic to that body of evidence, which thus, with the testimony also given by the results, at length lacks no characteristic necessary to prove the divinity of Christianity that we could reasonably require.

In addition, the miracles are themselves a revelation in a practical way, and speak most emphatically of the power, wisdom, and goodness, resident in Him by whom, or in whose name, they are wrought. We know practically the skill and knowledge that is possessed by an artist, or a mechanic, by the works which he produces. So is the power, goodness, etc., of Christ revealed by his miracles as well as by his words. Thus miracles add to and complete revelation, while they attest it. They fulfill our expectation of a practical display of the superhuman attributes of the Revealer, and, in perfect harmony with the superhuman nature of all his other manifestations, unite with them in majestically proclaiming him to be divine.

2d. But miracles are not an evidence merely of the completeness and the harmony of revelation within itself. They are, besides, themselves a separate and positive proof of the divinity of revelation. By their own superhuman character they convinced the men to whom revelation was first imparted that it was divine, and their accomplishment remains to us a solid and convincing evidence of the same great fact still. Peter, on the day of

Pentecost, only fifty days after Christ's death, in addressing the unbelieving Jews, and that in Jerusalem, boldly told them that "Jesus of Nazareth" had been "approved of God among you *by miracles, and wonders, and signs,* which God did by him in the midst of you, *as ye yourselves also know*" (Acts ii. 29). Paul, too, writing to the backsliding Galatians, some of whom had begun to deny his apostleship, could also confidently appeal to his miracles wrought among them, and say, "Truly the signs of an apostle were wrought among you in all patience, *in signs, and wonders, and mighty deeds*" (2 Cor. xii. 12). And our Lord himself said of those who had rejected him: "If I had not done among them the works which none other man did, they had not had sin; but now have they both seen and hated both me and my Father. But this cometh to pass that the word might be fulfilled that is written in their law, They hated me without a cause" (John xv. 24, 25). From these passages it appears that the Scriptures themselves represent miracles as signs by which His messengers were "approved of God" unto men; that without them those messengers, even Christ himself, might be rejected without "sin;" but that, having seen them, their rejecters had thereby "seen"—in the exhibitions of his omnipotence in working these miracles—"the Father," and therefore thenceforward they had no excuse for their rejection; they had had all-sufficient evidence; "they hated me without a cause." On account, therefore, of this conclusive nature of the evidence given by miracles, and because their reality could not *then* be disputed, our Lord and his apostles appealed to them in proof of their divine mission, with evidently the utmost confidence. Moreover, we find by the quotation of them made subsequently to their performance, by the Lord and the apostles, that the miracles remained for after-years also a standing proof of those claims, and, accordingly, we here present them as such.

This proof, however, does not arise merely from their character as "wonders" merely. The term "miracle," as used in the English version to denote the supernatural occurrences recorded in the Scriptures, is liable to mislead. It is from the Latin *miraculum*, meaning, simply, something wonderful, and perhaps it is generally understood to mean merely a marvelous thing. But the words used in the Bible to denote the miracles have a much larger meaning than that, and the words, both in the Hebrew and Greek, which mean merely "a wonder," are not those used to denote miracles. "No doubt all God's works are wonderful; but when the word is applied to his doings in the Bible, it is his works in nature that are generally so described. . . . But the word *wonder* is not the word in the Hebrew properly applicable to what we mean by miracles, and in the New Testament our Lord's works are never called 'miracles' (θαύματα) at all. The people are often said to have 'wondered' at Christ's acts; but those acts themselves were not intended simply to produce wonder—they had a specific purpose, indicated by the term properly applicable to them, and that term is *sign*. This is the sole Hebrew term for what we mean by *miracle;* but there are other words applied to our Lord's doings in the New Testament" (McClintock and Strong's Cyclopædia, Art. Miracles, Vol. VI., p. 310).

These latter words, as the same authority goes on to show, are *terata, dynameis, erga,* and *semeia.*

1. The first "is a term which approaches very nearly to our word miracle, and defined by Liddell and Scott, in their Greek Lexicon, as a '*sign, wonder, marvel,* used of any appearance or event in which men believed that they could see the finger of God.' But, with that marvelous accuracy which distinguishes the language of the Greek Testament, our Lord's works are never called *terata* in the Gospels."

It is used, however, in Acts ii. 19, and Heb. ii. 4, in reference to our Lord's works, and elsewhere frequently, to denote the works of the apostles.

2. *Dynameis* is the word from which we derive our word *dynamics*. It is "the most common term for our Lord's miracles" in the first three Gospels, and signifies *powers—i. e.*, faculties, or capacities, for doing something. "The teaching, therefore, of this word, *dynameis*, *powers*, or *faculties*, is that our Lord's works were perfectly natural and ordinary to him. They were his capacities, just as sight and speech are ours. Now, in a brute animal, articulate speech would be a miracle, because it does not lie within the range of its capacities; . . . it does lie within the compass of our faculties, and so in us it is no miracle. Similarly, the healing of the sick, the giving sight to the blind, the raising of the dead, etc.—things entirely beyond the range of our powers, yet lay entirely within the compass of our Lord's capacities, and were in accordance with the laws of his nature."

3. *Erga*, the next word, used almost wholly by John to denote our Lord's miracles, means *works*. "This term stands in a very close relation to the preceding word, *dynameis*, or *faculties*. A faculty, when exerted, produces an

10

ergon, or work. Whatever powers or capacities we have, whenever we use them, bring forth a corresponding result. . . . Now, had our Lord been merely a man, any and every work beyond the compass of men's powers would have been a miracle. . . . But the Gospel of John . . . is everywhere penetrated with the conviction that a higher nature was united in him to his human nature; . . . and so here. Our Lord's miracles to him are simply and absolutely *erga*, WORKS; but, as we have seen before, they are also divine works, 'works of God.' Still, in Christ, according to John's view, they were perfectly natural. They were the necessary and direct result of that divine nature which in him was indissolubly united with his human nature. The last thing which the apostle would have thought about them was that they were 'miraculous'—*i. e.*, *wonderful*. That God should give his only-begotten Son to save the world was wonderful. That such a Being should ordinarily do works entirely beyond the limits of man's powers did not seem to John wonderful, and hence the simple but deeply significant term (*works*) by which he characterizes them."

4. Finally, the fourth term, *semeia*, constantly also used by John, means *signs*. This may be regarded as the common generic term

applicable to all the supernatural works narrated in the Scriptures. "This is the sole Hebrew term for what we mean by *miracle*. . . .' The one proper term for miracle, throughout the whole Bible, is *semeion*, a sign" (McClintock and Strong). Now, John, in so frequently using this term along with that of *erga, works*, does not do so without a very significant meaning. "Such works [as we have considered above] were not wrought without a purpose; nor did such a Being come without having a definite object to justify his manifestation. . . . Now, John points this out in calling our Lord's works *semeia, signs*." This "tells us in the plainest language that these works were tokens calling the attention of men to what was then happening; and especially is it used in the Old Testament of some mark, or signal, confirming a promise, or covenant. Such a 'sign' God gave to Cain (Gen. iv. 15); . . . to Noah (Gen. ix. 13); . . . to Abraham (Gen. xvii. 11), . . . and to the Jews by the Sabbath-day (Ex. xxxi. 13; Ezek. xx. 12)," in pledge of his particular promises made to them, respectively. So also John (John ii. 11) calls the changing of water into wine at Cana "this beginning of *signs*" (not " miracles," as it is wrongly translated in the English version); and (John iv. 54) the healing of the centurion's son as "the second sign," "as being the first and second indications of Christ's wielding those powers which belong to God as the Creator and Author of nature, and which, therefore, pledged the God of nature, as the sole possessor of these powers, to the truth of any one's teaching who came armed with them." Therefore it was that the Jews asked for "a sign" (Matt. xii. 38; xvi. 1; John ii. 18; vi. 30), and some believed "when they saw the *signs* which he did" (John ii. 23); and Nicodemus, the "Pharisee" and "ruler," confessed, "Rabbi, we know that thou art a teacher come from God; for no man can do these *signs* that thou doest except *God* be *with him*" (John iii. 2). "Thus John's word shows that our Lord's *works* had a definite purpose. They were not wrought at random, but were intended for a special object. What this was is easy to tell. . . . The herald of a divine dispensation must have proof to offer that he does come from God, and such proof as pledges the divine attributes to the truth of his teaching. This is the reason why the Old Testament dispensation was one of *signs*. On special occasions justifying the divine interference, and in the persons of its great teachers, the prophets, supernatural proof was given in two ways. . . . The divine *omniscience* was pledged to the truth of their words by the prediction of future events, and his *omnipotence* by their working things beyond the ordinary range of nature. The Old Testament proofs of a revelation were prophecy and miracle. We can think of no others, and nothing less would suffice." Accordingly, Christ, as "the bearer to mankind of God's final and complete message," not only delivered prophecies, but wrought *works*, which were *signs* of his divine mission upon earth.

This is the true significance of what we call "miracles." "They are signs, *and* wonderful signs, *and* such wonderful signs as could not have been wrought by finite power" (Smith's Bible Dict., Art. Miracles, Vol. III., p. 1963). They are therefore proofs, and unmistakable proofs, of the presence of the power and authority of God attendant upon those who accomplished them, and thus they attest the divine character of the message which they professed to bring from God to men.

Such is the evidential force of miracles, wherever they may really exist. If, then, we can show also, beyond a reasonable doubt, that the accounts of them which we have in the Gospels are true, and that they were really wrought by Christ, the conclusion is inevitable that Christ was truly sent of God, and therefore that his religion is divine.

This proof has been already, in great measure, set forth in Part First, in the consideration given there (particularly in Chapter IV.) of the authenticity of the evidence. The possibility of miracles, and the competency of evidence to prove their occurrence, are also there shown. Our space will not allow us to restate that proof here. We must at this point be content with referring the reader back to it, if he wishes for a full view of all the argument in the case. Suffice it to say now, that for the actual occurrence of the miracles related of Christ, we have the concurrent and uncontradicted testimony of the New Testament writers, given in such a manner, and under such circumstances, as that, on every principle by which any testimony in any case is held to be valid, their testimony in this case must be received as true. In addition, however, to the evidence presented in Part First in support of this position, and which the reader is requested to review, at least before he passes an unfavorable judgment, we call attention to the considerations following:

1st. The circumstances under which they were wrought forbade mistake or deception (*vide* Leslie's "Four Tests," quoted in Watson's "Institutes," Part I., Ch. 12). (1) They were such as men's outward senses could judge of them. The feeding of the thousands in the desert from the few loaves and fishes, on two occasions, by Christ; his healing of the paralytic, of the man born blind, and of various lepers; his raising of the widow's son from the dead, and of Lazarus, who had been dead three days, until his body had become offensive; greatest of all, his own resurrection and ascension—these and others were things such as men could judge of by their senses, and not like many falsely alleged to be miracles—as, *e. g.*, that alleged by the papists of the bread and wine of the communion being changed into flesh and blood; for such a change is wholly imperceptible to any of the senses, but those of Christ appealed to the senses for the evidence of their reality—as it is reasonable to expect a miracle to do. (2) They were done publicly, in the face of the world. Many were wrought before accusers and enemies, and in the presence of vast numbers of men. In this they differ from all pretended miracles, which have usually been performed in private, and have not been witnessed by any but those directly concerned in them. (3) In the case of the miracle of the resurrection of Christ, the observance of the "first day of the week" as its memorial, became an institution of the Christian Church. It is a good proof of the reality of an event if we find an institution, originating in historical times, and of whose origin no other account can be given, still existing professedly as a memorial of that event. Such is the Christian Sabbath (*vide* Smith's Bible Dictionary, Art. "The Lord's Day"), and as such it remains a proof of the resurrection of our Lord. (4) Its observance was instituted directly after the resurrection (*vide* Smith, *ib.*, and cf. Acts ii. 7; 1 Cor. xvi. 1, 2; Heb. x. 25), when the proof against it, if false, was easily accessible, and when its observance would publicly and generally call attention—among the Jews especially, by the remarkable change of observance from the seventh to the first day of the week—to the false miracle alleged to have taken place on that day. Yet, though public notice was thus called to it, and though refutation would have been (as we shall see more fully in the next chapter) most easy, and though the Christians suffered the most bitter and violent hostility and persecution, yet the refutation was never given. "You may challenge all the world to show that any action is fabulous which has all four of these marks. The matters of fact — *e. g.*, of Mohammed, or what is fabled of the heathen deities—do all want some of them. First, for Mohammed—he *pretended to no miracles*, as he

tells us himself in the Koran (c. 6, etc.), and all those which are told of him do all want the first two marks; for his pretended journey to the moon, his night journey to Jerusalem, and thence to heaven, etc., were not performed before anybody, nor were they capable of being perceived by the senses of men. The same is true of the fables told of the heathen gods—as of Jupiter's turning himself into a bull, etc. Nobody ever saw it, and besides, the folly and unworthiness of such senseless pretended miracles are enough to condemn them. Again, the public observances—as the Bacchanalia, and other feasts, etc., instituted in commemoration of their deities—are not pretended to have begun at the time and place when the occurrences alleged to have given rise to them took place, but are acknowledged to have been first ordained by others in their memory ages afterward, when imposture was not so easily detected. And so as to the Romish miracles, reported to have been wrought by the saints, etc., since the days of the apostles—they all want the first marks. And besides, they usually are only 'such as make fools stare and wise men suspect;' and as they begin, so they end—in vain—in establishing nothing worthy."
—*Horne.* But the miracles of the Bible were not afraid of the open day, of scrutiny by en-

emies, and of trial by the senses. They left also an enduring memorial existing from the time of their occurrence, they had a wise and beneficent end, they were worthy of God, and they established the Christian Church. In all this they are without parallel in the records of the human race.

2d. The character of Christ's miracles in its very nature bears witness to their truth. Not only were they worthy of God's working, but we also have such evidence thereof as the following, viz.: (1) Their great number. Very many are individually mentioned. Many others are mentioned only generally and incidentally (*e. g.*, as in Matt. viii. 16, where it is said "they brought unto him many that were possessed with devils, and he cast out the spirits with his word, and healed all that were sick," etc.). (2) Their greatness. They were such as could not be feigned, but were such as satisfying the hunger of thousands from a few loaves and fishes, calming the winds and the sea, curing the lepers, and raising the dead. (3) Their simplicity. All were done without any ostentatious show. And they were done at a touch, by a word, with the utmost ease. (4) Their disinterestedness. None were performed for reward; none ever gained him any worldly benefit whatever. (5) Their effects in converting many incredulous persons, and even some enemies (as, *e. g.*, Paul), to embrace his doctrine. (6) "They were actually admitted as facts by the [early] opposers of Christianity: Celsus, and Hierocles, and Julian the Apostate, and the Jewish rabbis in the Talmud—all of whom wrote and argued bitterly against Christianity—have yet all left their acknowledgment of the actual occurrence of these events, accounting for them by magical arts, which Celsus affirms Christ must have learned in Egypt" (Johnson's Cyclopædia, Art. Miracles). (7) Their great variety, which yet, very remarkably, evidently constituted one organic whole. This forms a very striking view of the miracles, and therefore we have reserved it for the last, that we may give it more in full by appending an extract from Westcott ("Introduction to Gospels," App. E), who, to show their singular harmony, completeness, and unity, both in themselves and in the revelation they disclose, gives the following (tentative) classification:

I. *Miracles in Nature.*—1. Miracles of Creative Power. (*a*) Christ the Source of joy—the character of nature changed: the water made wine (John ii. 1–12). (*b*) Christ the Source of subsistence—substance increased: the bread multiplied (Matt. xiv. 15–21, etc.).

(*c*) Christ the Source of strength—force controlled: the walking on the water (Matt. xiv. 22–26, etc.). 2. Miracles of Providence. (*a*) Of Blessing. *a*. The founding of the outward Church: the first miraculous draught of fishes (Luke v. 1–11); *b*. The Defense of the Church without: the storm stilled (Matt. viii. 23–27, etc.); *c*. The Support of the Church from within: the *stater* in the fish's mouth (Matt. xvii. 24–27); *d*. The Church of the Future: the second miraculous draught of fishes (John xxi. 1–23). (*b*) Of Judgment: the fig-tree cursed (Matt. xxi. 19, etc.).

II. *Miracles on Man.*—1. Miracles of Personal Faith. (*a*) Organic Defects. *a*. Faith special: the two blind men in the house (Matt. ix. 29–31); *b*. Faith absolute: Bartimeus restored (Matt. xx. 29–34, etc.). (*b*) Chronic Impurity. *a*. Open leprosy (Matt. viii. 1–4, etc.); *b*. Secret: the woman with the issue (Matt. ix. 20–22). 2. Miracles of Intercession. (*a*) Organic Defects: the blind, and the deaf and dumb (Mark viii. 22–26; vii. 31–37). (*b*) Mortal Sicknesses. *a*. Fever: The nobleman's son healed (John iv. 46–54); *b*. Paralysis: The man borne of four (Matt. ix. 1–8). 3. Miracles of Love. (*a*) Organic Defect: the blind man healed (John ix.). (*b*) Disease. *a*. Fever (Matt. viii. 14, 15, etc.); *b*. Dropsy

(Luke xiv. 1–6); *c.* The withered hand (Matt. xii. 9–13); *d.* The impotent man (John v. 1–17); *e.* The spirit of infirmity (Luke xiii. 10–17). (*c*) Death. *a.* In the death-chamber: a girl raised (Matt. ix. 18, etc.); *b.* Upon the bier: a young man raised (Luke vii. 11–18); *c.* From the tomb: a tried friend raised (John xi.).

III. *Miracles Wrought on the Spirit-world.*— 1. Miracles of Intercession. (*a*) Simple intercession: the dumb man possessed by a devil (Matt. ix. 32–34; xii. 22, etc.). (*b*) Intercession based on natural ties: *a.* The Syrophenician's daughter (Matt. xv. 21–28, etc.); *b.* The lunatic boy (Matt. xvii. 14, etc.). 2. Miracles of Antagonism. (*a*) In the synagogue: the unclean spirit cast out (Mark i. 21–28, etc.). (*b*) In the tombs: the legion cast out (Matt. viii. 28–34).

This is totally different from all false miracles. In its completeness and unity it discloses, just as we should expect, the presence of God supernaturally working in the Person of Christ at *all* points, wherever it came into contact with human life and human circumstances, with unity and significance, with goodness and power—breaking forth, as we should expect it, on all occasions, and in all directions, wherever an occasion demanded its exercise, and giving us assurance in itself of its reality, and of the divine mission of Him whom it attended.

Thus, then, we assert the divinity of Christianity by the evidence of the miracles wrought by Christ. This, as to those miracles in general. There is one supereminent miracle, however, which is also the great corner-stone of Christian faith — the resurrection of Christ from the dead. Thus we will consider it in particular, not only as the "fundamental and crowning miracle of the gospel," and carrying with it the fact of its own existence as such the reality also of all the other miracles,* but also, in its single evidence, indisputably proving that Christ was sent of God.

---

*"In the resurrection," says Westcott, referring to his classification, given above, "all the forms of miraculous working are included. The course of nature was controlled, for there was a great earthquake; the laws of material existence were overruled, for when the doors were shut Jesus came into the midst of his disciples, and when their eyes were 'opened' he vanished out of their sight; the reign of death was overthrown, for many of the saints came out of their graves, and went into the holy city; the powers of the spiritual world were called forth, for angels watched at the sepulcher, and ministered to believers. Thus harmonious is the whole strain of Scripture. 'All things are double over against another, and God hath made nothing imperfect.'"

CHAPTER VII.

THE EVIDENCE OF MIRACLES—II. THE RESURRECTION OF CHRIST.

THE resurrection of Christ is one of the strongest proofs that we could ask of the divinity of Christianity. As such it was constantly cited by the apostles in proof of their doctrine, on the first preaching of the gospel. Peter, at Jerusalem, upon the day of Pentecost, less than two months after the resurrection, occupied a large part of his discourse with showing that, in fulfillment of prophecy, "this Jesus hath God raised up, whereof we are all witnesses" (Acts ii. 32), and that from this, and by his subsequent ascension and exaltation, and shedding forth the Holy Ghost, "therefore let all the house of Israel know assuredly, that God hath made that same Jesus, whom ye have crucified, both Lord and Christ" (verse 36); and so strong and convincing was this evidence, even to those who had crucified Christ, that "when they heard this, they were pricked in their hearts, and said unto Peter and the rest of the apostles, Men and brethren, what shall we do?" (verse 37). This will serve to show us the evidential value of miracles in general, and that of the resurrection of Christ in particular; and this value was not a mere temporary one, and confined to the time and place in which the resurrection had occurred, nor to the people who were familiar with the circumstances of its occurrence, but we find that Paul also, some twenty years afterward, at Athens, among a people as yet entirely unacquainted with any fact of Christianity, "preached unto them Jesus and the resurrection." And he preached it too as the evidence of the truth and authority of Christianity in calling men to repentance, saying, "And the times of this ignorance God winked at; but now commandeth all men everywhere to repent: because he hath appointed a day in the which he will judge the world in righteousness by that man whom he hath ordained; *whereof he hath given assurance unto all men in that he hath raised him from the dead*" (Acts xvii. 18, 30, 31). In another place (1 Cor. xv. 14) he elaborately sets it forth as a fact of the utmost importance to the assurance of our faith, declaring even, "And if Christ be not risen, then is our preaching vain, and your faith is also vain." Farther citation would be superfluous. In the Epistles of the New Testament alone (*vide* Angus's "Handbook," p. 360) there are more than fifty references to the resurrection of Christ, showing that it was considered as of special importance in the system of Christian doctrine. Its special importance as an Evidence fully appears in the above quotations, and accordingly we give it here a special prominence among the miracles as affording peculiar and irrefragable evidence of the divinity of the religion of Christ.

1. First we offer, over and above the general evidence already given for the truth of the facts contained in the Gospel narratives, the following special evidence in proof of the resurrection of Christ in particular:

(*a*) The disciples who gave their testimony could not have been deceivers in such a case, and have put forth an invented tale of his resurrection. 1st. No other explanation can be given of the disappearance of the body of Jesus. That he died by crucifixion is undoubted. The testimony of all the writers, even that of the heathen historian (*vide ante*, p. 94), is that he was so put to death. We have therefore the same proof of this as we have of any other fact recorded in Tacitus and those other writers. We take their statements as that of reliable historians who took pains to satisfy themselves, by competent evidence existing at the time they wrote, that the facts they recorded were true before they recorded them. Moreover, the Jews, who still remain the strong opposers of Christianity, and who at the time of his alleged resurrection had every means as well as every motive to expose such a deception, never doubted that he had died as a malefactor; and, as we shall subsequently see, in the very nature of the case, his death must necessarily have really occurred. What then became of his body? That it had disappeared from the tomb on the third day, notwithstanding the Jews had placed around it a guard of Roman soldiers to watch for three days, within which time they knew Christ had prophesied he should rise again, is also undoubted; for, if it were still in the tomb when the three days' watch had ended, then the Jews could have easily confounded the Christians by thus disproving by the soldiers this alleged fact, when they preached it in Jerusalem itself but a little more than a month afterward, and preached it too as being one of the very corner-stones of the Christian doctrine. Manifestly, a Christian Church, under such circumstances, could never have been formed in Jerusalem; nor could thus a convert have ever been made of an ardent Jewish enemy there, as acute and able as Saul of Tarsus. Yet it cannot be questioned that a Christian Church was formed in Jerusalem, and continued to exist there, despite the utmost persecutions; and it is certain, also, that Saul was at length convinced—by the evidence of this very resurrection — of the truth of the Christian religion, and became a convert. The two facts then so minutely and harmoniously related in the Gospels, of the death of Jesus, and of the disappearance afterward of his body, are true. What then became of the body? The Christians say that Jesus rose from the dead, and afterward ascended into heaven—the Jews, that his disciples had come by night, and stole his body away. These are the only two explanations offered, and are doubtless the only two possible to be offered. Since the dead body of Jesus had disappeared from the sealed tomb in which it had been placed, despite the soldiers guarding it, it must either have been stolen away, or he must have risen from the dead. The evidence shows that we cannot accept the former explanation, and that the latter therefore is the true and only conclusion.

1. It is highly improbable, in the nature of the case, that the former explanation is true. (1) It is improbable, because the terror under which the disciples evidently were at the time, as well as the fewness of their numbers; the

fact that they were taken by surprise by the crucifixion of Jesus taking place so soon after his triumphant entry into Jerusalem; the fact that the mass of the people were against them, and *all* the authorities—all this would have deterred them from even planning such an attempt against a band of the dreaded Roman soldiers, and, in all likelihood, would have prevented them from succeeding, if they had made the attempt. (2) The time and place, and the other circumstances, were very unfavorable for the success of such an attempt. The time was that of the Passover, in which there is always a full moon; the city and its suburbs were unusually crowded with people come up to attend the Passover; the sepulcher was just outside the city walls, and there was a guard of Roman soldiers, for whom it was death to sleep upon their post, set around the sepulcher itself. It was highly improbable, if even they could succeed in penetrating to the cave, that they could ever have borne off the body without being seen. (3) But if they had, they could scarcely have succeeded in disposing of it in concealment where it would not have been discovered, either by chance, or by the officers searching for it. The difficulty of doing so in criminal cases, even when the crime has been for some time unknown, and where the criminal has had the facilities of a lonely neighborhood, and the aid of modern scientific knowledge to help him, is well known. Scarce any such criminal escapes ultimate detection. A human body is very difficult to dispose of. But we are to suppose that these disciples, almost all of them Galileans, and therefore comparatively strangers in Jerusalem, ignorant of all scientific means of getting rid of the body, and in a crowded city and neighborhood, could do what criminals with every opportunity find it so hard to do, and effectually conceal the body, *though they had been previously suspected of an intention to commit the theft, and the theft had, immediately after its commission, been discovered.* (4) But if they had succeeded in doing it, why were they not at once arrested for the theft? They continued to stay in the city at least fifty days afterward, and even boldly preached publicly the *resurrection* of Jesus, the very doctrine against which their enemies had taken such extraordinary precautions. They thus rendered themselves peculiarly obnoxious to the Jewish authorities, by charging them, in this way, with basely killing their own Messiah. By publicly proving the falsity of the alleged resurrection, on the evidence of the soldiers, and by their arrest, trial, and conviction, the priests and scribes could have forever triumphantly destroyed that hated Christian sect—a sect which they did attempt with all their power to destroy by the most dreadful *persecution*. Yet, though the apostles were more than once arrested, they were never arrested for this crime; though other charges were brought against them before the legal tribunals, this one never was. But, moreover, if the Jews neglected this, why did the Romans do so? They were a people jealous in the extreme for the dignity of Rome. The disciples, if they stole the body, had broken the Roman seal which had been placed upon the stone, and they thus had committed an indignity and a crime against the Roman Government. Yet they were allowed to go free in the city undisturbed, and no proceedings whatever were had against them, by either Jews or Romans.

(5) Again, it is exceedingly improbable that so many men, inured to watching in the open air, should have fallen asleep *at once;* or if they did, that with all the noise unavoidably made in removing the "great stone" which had been used to stop up the entrance to the tomb, and in bearing forth the body of a full-grown man —requiring several men—through the midst of the soldiers, not *one* should have been aroused and discover the thieves. (6) And finally, it is most improbable that, if they had

all thus fallen asleep, they could have escaped punishment. No nation has ever had stricter discipline than the Romans. It was death for a soldier to sleep upon his post. Yet we hear nothing of any punishment awarded them for their flagrant breach of discipline. It is not likely that the Roman officers would for any reason have remitted their punishment; still more unlikely is it that the soldiers would have accused themselves in returning such a report of their conduct in explanation of the disappearance of the body.

2. But if their account is true, it is certain that it cannot be known to be true; for, be it remembered, upon the testimony of these deniers of the resurrection themselves, there were *no* actual witnesses of the theft, except the thieves themselves. The Jews were not there; the soldiers, as it is claimed, were asleep —if any one but the thieves had beheld it, they would certainly have arrested them and aroused the soldiers. Then how can it be proved that the body was stolen? If the soldiers were asleep when the body left the tomb, then all that they can truly testify to is, that when they awoke they found the tomb broken open and the body gone. But they cannot say how; and so, though they had slept, the resurrection, so far as that is concerned, might have

taken place. But if they were awake, why did they not prevent the theft?

3. In opposition to this improbable, inconsistent, yea, evidently false, account, we have the only other reasonable explanation—given directly, clearly, and consistently, by all the disciples—that after his death they saw him again, alive; that they talked, ate, and otherwise associated with him, at intervals, for forty days; and that he himself, who was so perfectly truthful and holy, assured them again and again, and gave them bodily proofs of the truth of his assertion, that he had really risen from the dead, even as it had been foretold, and as it "behooved him" to do. (1) In the Jews' explanation of the disappearance of his body, we have just seen an instance of the extreme difficulty of forging without detection a tale consistent with the circumstances and with itself, even by those possessed of the greatest advantages of power, learning, etc. Greenleaf has also pointed out (*vide ante*, p. 106) the almost impossibility of doing it. But could the humble disciples, powerless and unlearned as they were, have been able to forge a tale about so remarkable a matter as not to be inconsistent, and therefore open to exposure by enemies, who, being in power, had every means of detection at their command, as

they had every motive to prompt them to use those means? Yet neither they nor the most acute minds, during the centuries since, have ever been able to show the forgery in the least degree. (2) The disciples, we are told, were themselves very incredulous, and "slow to believe" the fact. (3) They had no motive to utter such a falsehood. There was no fame, or riches, or power, to be gained in this world by it, and surely they could expect in the next nothing but punishment for such a stupendous and blasphemous falsehood. Only dangers, persecutions, torture, exile, and death, awaited them here from preaching the resurrection, and, if false, eternal ruin after death. Is it conceivable that any man would be so carried away by madness as to dare all this in support of a known, monstrous, and incredible lie? It is inconceivable that so many men, through so many years, with such perfect unanimity, and under such sufferings, should persist in doing so. (4) But had they all, nevertheless, so agreed, it is still improbable that they would have ventured to publish this forged account, as the apostles did in Jerusalem, in the very place, and immediately after the time, in which the thing thus falsely alleged was said by them to have taken place. They might have gone to a distant country and waited many years, but forgers such as these would scarcely have dared to utter their forgery in the very place where their enemies were most numerous and powerful, and where every facility for exposing and punishing them existed. (5) If they had madly ventured to take this last improbable step, it is impossible to believe that they could ever have so successfully escaped detection and exposure. Let it be remembered that no such exposure was ever made; yet they repeated their statements over and over again, sometimes separately, sometimes together. They were at various times arrested and examined before the very highest legal tribunals, both Jewish and Roman, by men trained to the business of detecting and punishing crime, and whose imperative official duty it was to do so; and those authorities had the greatest motives for punishing them, and no motive for shielding them. Nevertheless, there was never found any discrepancy in their testimony, and there was never any conviction secured for this crime, nor any punishment awarded for it. (6) Lastly, the general character of the apostles forbids us from suspecting them of such a forgery. Their character has never been impugned. Their whole history, as well as the whole tenor of their spirit, manifested in their writings that remain to us, show them to be men of the most undoubted purity, benevolence, and truth. They were incapable of designedly framing so false and misleading a story, even had they been able; and their united, positive, and life-long testimony to the resurrection of Christ, with no *evidence* against it, is entitled to be received as a true relation of the facts they attest.

Since, then, it is, in the first place, so highly improbable, in the nature of the case, that the disciples could have stolen the body of Jesus; since, also, if they had, it could not have been known, but, at the utmost, only suspected; and since, too, we have the positive, continued, concurring, and uncontradicted testimony of so many witnesses of the highest character to the reality of the Lord's resurrection, we must, in all fairness, believe that Christ *was* seen by the apostles after his crucifixion, and that they were entirely innocent of all forgery in their testimony to this fact, and of all intention to deceive.

(*b*) But neither were they self-deceived. Modern objectors, seeing the hopelessness of proving them deceivers, have fallen upon the theory of self-deception, in the case of the apostles, in order to explain the facts. In answer, we present the following arguments condensed from Row ("Christian Evidences," etc.):

From the Pauline and the other Epistles of the New Testament it is proved—

1. That it is an unquestionable fact that the Church which had been for the time dissolved at the crucifixion was reconstructed on the basis of the resurrection.

2. That the belief in it originated on the spot, and within a few days of the crucifixion, and that the fact was openly proclaimed then and there as the new foundation on which the Church was to be erected and the Messiahship of Jesus to be set up.

3. That all the efforts of Paul and his fellow-persecutors failed to discover that this belief was the result of fraud or delusion.

4. That the apostolic body believed that they had two interviews with Jesus, in which they saw him alive after his crucifixion.

5. That two of the apostles were persuaded that they had two private interviews with him.

6. That upward of five hundred brethren believed that they saw him alive after his crucifixion, when they were assembled in a body.

7. That Paul was persuaded that he had seen him.

8. That large numbers of believers were firmly persuaded that, in consequence of his resurrection, they had become possessed of certain supernatural gifts and endowments.

9. That the belief in the resurrection acted as a mighty power of moral and spiritual regeneration.

These facts effectually disprove — 1. Every form of the theory of their mythic or legendary origin; 2. That it is impossible that the belief in the resurrection could have grown up in the gradual manner in which ordinary fictions do, at distant times and places; 3. That until some other equally rational account, affording an adequate explanation of all the subsequent historical facts of the Christian Church, can be propounded, we are fully entitled to accept this, the account which the Church has ever put forward as the true one, and the sole ground of its existence.

(*a*) To give such an explanation, the theory of "visions" has been advanced — viz., that Christ never rose from the dead, but that some one or more of his enthusiastic followers fancied they saw him alive, and mistook the creation of their distempered imaginations for an actual resurrection, and succeeded in persuading the other disciples that he was risen from the dead. These, in turn, also took to seeing visions of the risen Jesus, and fancying not only that they had interviews with him, but that they received his orders to reconstruct his Church on the basis of his resurrection, etc. The attempt was made, succeeded, and the Church—the greatest of institutions—was erected on this foundation of baseless delusions by a few credulous fanatics. But this is impossible; for—

1st. The disciples could not have even expected it. 1. The disciples, immediately after the crucifixion, were in a state of deepest depression. 2. The idea of resurrection was one utterly foreign to all ancient thought, so that however men might have supposed they had seen spirits, the very thought of a body being raised from the dead would never have occurred to them. 3. The disciples did not so understand Jesus when he predicted it, as appears from the same account which tells of the prediction. Therefore they were not expecting it, but were filled with the prepossession and fixed idea of his death and the utter ruin of his cause; yet, expectancy, prepossession, and fixed idea, are well established by mental physiologists as the necessary mental states to enable even enthusiastic and credulous persons to mistake subjective impressions for external realities (*vide* Carpenter's "Mental Physiology"). But since we know that a great change, nevertheless, occurred in the minds of the disciples in a few days, *contrary* to their expectation; since, also, the Church was reconstructed on new conceptions of the Messiah—*i. e.*, of a spiritual and invisible Messiah, instead of one visible and temporal—we infer that Jesus was actually raised from the dead.

2d. But suppose that Mary—a woman—did first fancy she saw him alive, and that she conversed with him, and that he promised to meet her again, and that she fancied that he did again meet her, so that her delusion did not vanish; suppose she had such a series of ideal visions and conversations—yet how could she have communicated her delusions to the other disciples, so that they too would begin to imagine that they saw the Lord, talked, walked, and ate, with him, and touched him, at various times and in different places—*i. e.*, not a spirit, but the veritable flesh and bones of his body —and that he made engagements for other interviews with them, and kept them? And this too in a few days after his crucifixion, and when his body really lay near by, corrupting in the grave? and that therefore they forthwith proceeded to reconstruct the Church on this foundation, and did greatly succeed in building up the most wonderful and enduring institution among men on this airy delusion of their fancies? and that they *all* concurred in this same identical delusion? Even among lunatics a concurrence in their hallucinations is unknown.

It is asserted, however, that Mohammed succeeded in erecting his Church on such a basis of supposed appearances. Now, there is much to warrant the conclusion that Mohammed was, in part at least, a conscious impostor; but the most that can be said is that he undertook his thirteen years' mission at Mecca under the persuasion that he had received a divine commission through the angel. Here note: 1. That there was no resurrection—an idea not natural to the human mind—but an angelic appearance, the idea of which is familiar and common to enthusiasts; 2. There is no testimony of the matter but that of himself; 3. It was not capable of refutation, as that of the resurrection of a body recently dead would have been by the production of the body; 4. Mohammed, in point of fact, never did found his Church on such a peaceful basis. It was only, after thirteen years, when he grasped the sword that he had any success; and if he had continued his endeavor to found his Church by peaceful means only, the Church of Mohammed would never have existed.

3d. But suppose all these impossible things, there yet remains to account for St. Paul's extraordinary delusion, that he too had seen the risen Lord, talked with him, received directions as to his future conduct from him, etc.

(*vide* Acts ix. 1–6, 11; 1 Cor. xv., etc.), so that from a most violent persecutor of the Church of Christ he suddenly became its most laborious missionary, and devoted his whole afterlife in self-sacrifice to the service of his Master. The 27th chapter of Acts, as well as the preceding chapters, prove, beyond the shadow of a doubt, that the author of the Acts was a companion of Paul. Without doubt, he must have received the account of Paul's conversion from Paul himself, and therefore, in the circumstances thus recorded, we have Paul's own account of the occurrences which led to his conversion, as he himself believed them. Now, how came he to believe in such a delusion—he in whom there could be absolutely no expectancy, and in whom the prepossession and the fixed idea, that Jesus was a wicked and dangerous *Impostor*, had previously wrought so strongly as to impel him to the most violent persecution—a persecution which he was then on his way to accomplish? How, we say, could he, against all his mental prepossessions and ideas, have so suddenly, completely, and permanently, fallen under such a ·delusion? Nay, so much so as to believe himself blind for three days, and at the end of that time to feel "as it were scales fall from his eyes," and immediately and ever after, at the peril of his life, unceasingly to labor to build up that cause which he had formerly tried to destroy—he, a man of the soundest reason, the acutest mental discrimination, and the highest education and cultivation?

(*b*) The only alternative left to unbelief is the theory that Jesus did not die, but fell into a state of syncope, which was mistaken for death, and in that state he was taken down from the cross, and put into the sepulcher, from which he gradually recovered, and thus appeared again to his disciples. But—1. Such an account never was heard of at the time by the enemies of our Lord, nor since, till modern times; 2. His body was in the custody of the Romans and Jews; 3. He had undoubtedly been greatly exhausted by his agony in the garden, his loss of rest throughout the previous night, the excitement of his various trials, the weariness of prolonged exertion, lasting from the evening before up to the hour of his crucifixion, and by his scourging; 4. After all this, he hung several hours on the cross, and at length was pierced in the side by a spear; 5. Afterward, he was laid for about thirty-six hours in a cold sepulcher, bound up with spices, in bandages and wrappings. It is incredible that a man could have lived through all this; yet, in addition, he must also have succeeded in freeing himself from his bandages, in rolling away the stone from the mouth of the sepulcher, and in reaching the house of some friend in safety, where he slowly recovered in secret. But, farther, this supposes—6. That the disciples who saw him mistook a slow recovery from extreme exhaustion and painful wounds for a triumphant resurrection; 7. That during his recovery, which must have taken a long time, and which must have been kept a profound secret, the rest of the disciples still kept together, and did not give way to discouragement and despair, but, when at last he was well, were ready, after so long a time, to accept the belief that he had risen from the dead; 8. And that they had seen him alive a few days after his resurrection; 9. And that Paul too, the persecutor, who, in inflicting his persecutions, must have heard and disbelieved the story, yet afterward imagined he had seen him in a flash of lightning, which felled him to the earth, and made him blind for three days; 9. That the apostles believed they had at length seen him leave the world, and go up to heaven; 10. That they forthwith proceeded to reconstruct the Church on this *new* conception of an invisible and spiritual Messiah; 11. And that they did, on this delusion, actually rear up the greatest and best institution that has ever existed among men.

We conclude that the disciples were neither deceivers nor self-deceived, but that the resurrection of our Lord Jesus Christ is a most certain fact. As such, it manifests the superhuman and divine character of Christianity, being itself one of the essential facts upon which Christianity is built, and from which it derives its strength.* Moreover, it establishes

---

* To appreciate this more fully, and also to see the harmonious unity of the several facts which form the foundation of the Christian religion, and especially to note how the fact of the resurrection, followed by the ascension of our Lord, gives completion, while it imparts fresh life and meaning, to all the other great facts, let us remember—1. That not only did it, as a miracle alone, give proof of the divine mission of Christ, but also as a miracle *in fulfillment of prophecy.* In Ps. xvi. 10 it had been predicted as a sign of the Messiah—"Thou wilt not leave my soul in hell [*i. e.,* in the grave]; neither wilt thou suffer thine Holy One to see corruption"—and accordingly, Peter, on the day of Pentecost, to the murderers of Christ, used this with most convincing effect, as a proof of the Messiahship of Christ. (*Vide* Acts ii. 25–31.) 2. It proved his divinity—"Declared to be the Son of God with power, . . . by the resurrection from the dead" (Rom. i. 4). 3. It completed the work of redemption; for—1st. It showed that his death was by way of atonement, and not of necessity, and proved what Christ had said of himself as the good Shepherd, "I lay down my life . . . that I might take it again. . . . No man taketh it from me, but I lay it down of myself. I

the general fact of miracles by Christ, and, taken with the testimony of the disciples to the other miracles, proves them also to have been really wrought.

As such, the miracles display the wisdom, the power, and the goodness of Christ, and so constitute an harmonious part of that revelation which he came to give, while also they add their own witness to all the other testimonies, to form together an inexpugnable evidence of the divinity of his religion.

---

have power to lay it down, and I have power to take it again" (John x. 15–18). In this, as also in that by his resurrection, God's acceptance was shown of his sacrifice on the cross as fully sufficient an atonement for man, we understand how "he was delivered for our offenses, and *raised again for our justification*" (Rom. iv. 25). 2d. It showed him to be the Conqueror and Destroyer of "him that had the power of death—that is, the devil." 3d. It was needful for his ascension, and the fulfillment of his great offices of Intercessor and High-priest, of sending forth the Holy Ghost, and of "preparing a place" for his people. 4. It was the proof, the pattern, and the pledge, of our own resurrection from the grave. Thus we see the importance of this great fact to the Christian system, the perfect correspondence of this fact to all the rest, and the perfect completeness in the supply it thus furnishes of the whole. This harmony and perfection is found in no other system, for no other is the complete revelation of God.

CHAPTER VIII.

THE SUPERNATURAL RESULTS.

FINALLY, we point to the Results of Christianity—the superhuman moral force and power it has wielded for good in the world—in evidence of its divinity. This is the last criterion that can be applied, and to this final test of experiment—the crucial touch-stone of modern science—Christianity, having passed the ordeal of all other trials of its truth, fears not to be tried by this last means of determination, but gladly challenges its examination also.

This too is a practical test capable of being applied in every generation and by every man. It is one, also, that is as really convincing to-day, to the candid and reflecting mind, as miracles were in the days of the apostles, and as sure a token of the presence of divine energy attending the gospel of Christ. "And now" (*i. e.*, in these days), says Augustin, in his sermon on "The Recovery of Sight to the Blind," referring to Christ, "he worketh greater cures, *on account of which* he disdained not then to exhibit those lesser ones—*i. e.*, curing the blind, etc. For as the soul is better than the body, so is the saving health of the soul better than the health of the body. The blind body doth not now open its eyes by a miracle of the Lord, but the blinded heart openeth its eyes to the word of the Lord. The mortal corpse doth not now rise again, but the soul which lay dead in a living body."

Indeed, as Van Oosterzee points out, "This testimony can be shown in its full force only when the kingdom of God shall have been completed. . . . Think of the blessed influence of Christianity on family life, society, the State, civilization, art, science, philosophy—the entire life of man and mankind—and, besides, of all which the history of missions tells us of the renewing power of the word of truth. Nor must we forget how a great part of the most precious of the seed is hidden from the short-sighted eye, yet is every now and then revealed in a surprising manner. And then, after all, ask where we can find a parallel to what, in all these respects, the history of God's kingdom proclaims. Still, though a full knowledge of the benefits produced by Christianity can thus never be known till eternity, we nevertheless know sufficient of its potent influence for good, both in the past and present, over savages and philosophers, to show its incomparable superiority over all other moral systems, and such as prove it to be divine."

I. First we appeal to the personal experience of *all* that have ever sincerely tried Christianity. This, we say, is the test of experiment, boasted by science as the infallible criterion, without the proof of which no theory is to be received. But then, on the other hand, no theory ought to be rejected that does possess this proof. We therefore cheerfully submit the claims of our religion to this method of verification, only demanding that it be faithfully used by objectors for themselves if they will, or if they will not even make trial of it themselves, that they will at least give a candid reception of, and belief in, the testimony of those who have done so. We ask attention, therefore, to the following facts:

1. ALL who have embraced Christianity, in every age and country, comprising millions of souls of every race, condition, sex, and age, have testified that Christianity is true. It is doubtful whether, of the millions who have once embraced it, however even they may have afterward relapsed into wickedness, any can be produced, either from the history of the past, or the multitudes of the present, who voluntarily have said, or will say, that they have honestly tried Christianity, and found it

to be false. Certain it is that the overwhelming majority will testify to the contrary, and declare that they have found it gloriously true. And the exceptions—if exceptions there be—may be rationally explained in the same way as we account for those no less exceptional experimenters in science who separately differ from the great body of their brethren as to the results of some experiment—viz., because of inaccuracy of observation, the influence of some particular theory of theirs, etc. Nor are such rare exceptions to weigh in our estimation any more in one case than the other. The vast preponderating testimony of the other side must be accepted as the only true testimony given by science as to the result of the experiment in question, and it must be so accepted also as the real evidence in the matter of religion.

2. These witnesses (*vide* Horne's "Introduction") have testified plainly and strongly; they have continued their testimony through life; they have done so frequently, when thereby they drew upon themselves disgrace, imprisonment, and cruel death; and they have done so often, when, by renouncing their principles, they might have enjoyed much of this world's fame and fortune. They have therefore given the strongest proofs possible of their

real convictions, and of their belief in the religion of Jesus Christ.

3. They say that Christianity does for them what it promises to do; that God does answer prayer; that the Holy Spirit is given them through Christ; that their moral natures are regenerated; their souls have a joy, and comfort, and strength, such as the world knows not of; they have love for God and man, they have purity and truth, when before there was malice and hate, uncleanness and falseness; that it does support in the hour of trial and of death, and that it is by far the most precious possession that they have or can have, and that they would much rather part with life itself than with it.

4. For the reality of this change from their former state, wrought in them, they affirm that they have the testimony of their own consciousness, which no one can deny, and that that consciousness is as clear as that of their own being, so that they can no more doubt it than they can their own being. They point also, confidently, to their changed outward lives, in which those that before were proud are now humble; those that were wrathful are now mild; those that were ambitious, avaricious, and sensual, selfish and full of hate, are now unworldly, generous, spiritual, self-

sacrificing, and loving. And for the truth of this they challenge the testimony of those around them, of enemies as well as friends.

5. Farther, this change is not only a change of character from what they themselves were before—it is a change also from the general character of the mass of all other men besides, especially from the general character of the human race *wherever* Christianity has exerted *no* influence. So that all the self-sacrificing efforts made in the world for the elevation and improvement of the human family—as by reformers, missionaries, preachers, etc.—all the reformatory and charitable institutions of the world—are almost, if not altogether, without an exception, the work of Christian charity, and not that of pagans, Mohammedans, or infidels.

6. These witnesses are of the most diverse countries and races, and of every age of the world since Christ. Among them are many who were at first averse, and even hostile, to Christianity, and who did their utmost to destroy it—as, *e. g.*, Paul and those converted on the day of Pentecost, the ancient and modern heathen, and many of our own day and country, who were once skeptics, but who afterward bore witness that they were before in error. Some of them too are men of the very highest

and best-trained powers of mind that have ever been known, and that too of every class of intellect. Philosophers, statesmen, poets, scientists—a Paul, a Justin, a Bacon, a Newton—Leibnitz, Shakespeare, Milton, Faraday, Agassiz, Maury, and a host of other of the most illustrious men, join in testifying their firm belief in Christianity.

Such testimony, continued through so many centuries, is sufficient to establish, on any reasonable ground of evidence, the truth of any proposition; but if, as we have seen is the case with Christianity, there is, on the other hand, *absolutely no adverse testimony*, we *must* accept it as true. At any rate, to reject it against this concurrent positive testimony of those who have put it to the practical test of trial, on the ground of any *a priori* reasoning, not to speak of prepossession or prejudice, is to the last degree unscientific and absurd. There is but one way, under such circumstances, to disprove it—viz., by making a fair and candid trial of it personally. To such a test Christianity continually invites all men, even her enemies. "Prove me now herewith, saith the Lord of hosts, if I will not open you the windows of heaven, and pour you out a blessing, that there shall not be room enough to receive it." "Christianity," says Coleridge, "is not a theory or a speculation, but a life; not a philosophy of life, but *a* life, and a living process. To the inquiry, How is this to be proved? I answer, TRY IT. It has been eighteen hundred years in existence, and has one individual left a record like the following: I tried it, and it did not answer? Have you ever met with any such person in whom you could put full confidence? Has it been your own experience? If neither your own experience nor the history of almost two thousand years has presented a single testimony to this purport, and if you have yourself met with some one in whom, on any other point, you would place unqualified trust, who, on his own experience, made report to you that he is faithful who promised, and what he promised he has proved himself able to perform, is it bigotry if I fear that the unbelief which prejudges and prevents the experiment with you has its source elsewhere than in the uncorrupted judgment; that not the strong, free mind, but the enslaved will, is the true, original infidel in this instance?"

II. The wonderful results flowing from the influence of Christianity are proved also by the great changes it has manifestly wrought in the world at large. Convincing as is the personal testimony of those who have made trial of the religion of Christ, we are not confined in our inquiry as to what are its actual results to their witness alone. The history also of the past, and the state of the world to-day, prove beyond controversy the unrivaled greatness of those results, both in the depth, the wide extent, and the permanence of the changes wrought, in proportion to the worldly means that it used, and in the amount of good produced by them. In both respects those results are utterly unapproached in the history of mankind; and while thus they indubitably confirm the testimony of Christians as to their personal experience of the effects of Christianity upon the lives of men, it also itself shows that those effects are far above merely human power, and therefore are divine.

1. The history of the early growth and progress of Christianity strikingly manifests this.

(1) Under the fiercest persecutions during the first three hundred years of its history, and though it used no worldly means whatever, but constantly taught doctrines of humility, unworldliness, and unselfishness — doctrines the most repugnant to human nature — the Church of Christ, nevertheless, against the most powerful and hostile systems of religion, and all the civil and military power of Rome arrayed against it, grew on, till, from a score

or two of despised Jews, it became at last the national Church of the vast Roman empire, then comprising nearly the whole known world, and containing some one hundred and twenty million people.

(2) Its promulgators thus "induced multitudes of *various* nations, Romans, Greeks, and barbarians, of diverse manners and languages, to forsake the religion of their ancestors; to desert ceremonies defended with vigor and authority, sanctified by remote age, and offering the most alluring gratification of the passions, to embrace doctrines pure and spiritual, whose severe discipline nature still opposes and shrinks from, whose high mysteries the pride of man prompts him to reject, and whose profession required them to reject almost every opinion hitherto held sacred, and exposed them to fierce and unpitying persecution, even unto death." Yet did the Church continue mightily to increase.

(3) It has since continually increased in numbers and in influence. The following table, taken from a late publication, and purporting to be the work of the historian, Sharon Turner, is perhaps very nearly correct, and shows substantially the rate of increase of the adherents to Christianity, up to the seventeenth century—viz.:

First century	500,000
Second century	2,000,000
Third century	5,000,000
Fourth century	10,000,000
Fifth century	15,000,000
Sixth century	20,000,000
Seventh century	24,000,000
Eighth century	30,000,000
Ninth century	40,000,000
Tenth century	50,000,000
Eleventh century	70,000,000
Twelfth century	80,000,000
Thirteenth century	75,000,000
Fourteenth century	80,000,000
Fifteenth century	100,000,000
Sixteenth century	125,000,000

Since the sixteenth century Christianity has increased still more marvelously, until now Johnson's Cyclopædia (Art. Christianity) gives the numbers of Christians, in 1872, throughout the world, at 380,000,000.

It is no slight evidence of its truth, and of its divinity, that it has through so many centuries not only survived the attack of so many successive enemies from without, and even the frequent betrayals of hypocrites and traitors within, but has steadily expanded under all disadvantages, in an irresistible progress throughout the world. All other systems, at most, have spread through one race only, or a few kindred races in blood, or contiguous in local habitation; all others have become stagnant, and at last faded away before the light of civilization. Christianity, in perfect contrast with them all, has spread with equal ease through the most diverse and distant races, continues with ever-increasing energy to subjugate the nations, and never has appeared so great and powerful as in the unrivaled light of the civilization of the present day; so that, while polytheism was rejected by all the leaders of thought of ancient Greece and Rome, when they had become enlightened, Christianity has still received the homage of the greatest intellects, and in the present generation has commanded the assent of such mighty minds as those of a Humboldt, a Faraday, and an Agassiz; and all this progress, be it remembered, has been without the use of worldly power or influence. By missionaries, under the severest deprivations and persecutions, have all her advances almost altogether been won, and not by the power of the sword, or by the use of worldly inducements. All these have opposed themselves to her; nevertheless, she has triumphed, and still triumphs, over them all. On the other hand, no other system among men—no philosophy, no scheme of morals, no educational system, no religion—has ever, even when backed by the rewards of this life and the power of kings, had such general, such permanent, and such continued success. Truly, Christianity is above all that is merely human —it is divine.

2. This influence of Christianity has exerted over man a superhuman power for *good*.

(1) As Christlieb has shown, all our modern culture is essentially the product of Christianity. Our written language even, through the influence of the Bible, has been largely affected and changed by it. Our arts and sciences— music, painting, sculpture, architecture, and the modern sciences—took their rise, respectively, from the devotion and from the spirit of free inquiry developed by Christianity; and our modern views in relation to marriage and the family life, our conceptions of right and order, and our habits of assiduous labor, are derived from its teachings; so that it is impossible to rend asunder our culture and the Christian religion; and therefore, in whatever degree the former is valuable, credit must be given to the latter for its good influences.

(2) The same author has also pointed out that a high and permanent civilization can never be wrought out upon any other principles than those of Christianity. That principle, so unknown to all other religions, as it is, and *because* it is, also to all the natural im-

pulses of human nature, but which is the fundamental principle of Christianity—viz., the principle of pure benevolence, or love to all, as opposed to selfishness, alienation, and hate —must necessarily form the basis of all high and enduring advancement in human culture. The following quotation, also taken from a contemporary secular journal, well shows this: "No candid observer will deny that whatever good there may be in our American civilization, it is the product of Christianity. Still less can he deny that the grand motives which are working for the elevation and purification of our society are strictly Christian. The immense energies of the Christian Church, stimulated by the love that shrinks from no obstacle, are all bent toward this great aim of universal purification. These millions of sermons and exhortations, which are a constant power for good; these countless prayers and songs of praise, on which the heavy-laden lift their hearts above the temptations and the sorrows of the world—are all the product of faith in Jesus Christ. That which gives us protection by day and night—the dwellings we live in, the clothes we wear, the institutions of social order—all these are the direct offspring of Christianity. All that distinguishes us from the pagan world, all that makes us what we are, and all that stimulates us in the task of making us better than we are, is Christian. A belief of Jesus Christ is the very fountain-head of every thing that is desirable and praiseworthy in our civilization, and this civilization is the flower of time. Humanity has reached its noblest thrift, its grandest altitudes of excellence, its high-water mark, through the influence of this faith."

(3) Christianity is the only hope of the *present* heathen world. Just as it was the only means which rescued the ancient heathens from the deep abyss of depravity and misery into which they had sunk, so now, if Christianity is not able to regenerate the present heathens of Asia and Africa, there is no other power that offers to do it. Those who object to Christianity would do well to ask themselves whether skepticism will rescue the degraded millions of India, and China, and barbarous Africa; or, if they have any plan, or are ready to put in operation any effort, to save them from the degradations and miseries of their abject superstitions. If not, and if Christianity cannot, then the larger part of the inhabitants of the earth are abandoned to hopeless despair. Commerce, unattended by Christianity, cannot do it. Bare commerce, undertaken, as it is, only for the purposes of

gain, and in many ways ministering to the evil passions of men—trading in the intoxicating liquors, the opium, etc., desired by the debased habits and tastes of savages and half-civilized nations—bare commerce, exhibiting at best the lower appetites of men, and too frequently carried on through wicked men, can do nothing of itself to refine and elevate them. Whatever is so done must be from the occasional and incidental association which those heathen may meet in commerce with men of superior character and habits, from Christian lands. But such men are superior to the heathen only because they do belong to Christian nations, and have, to a greater or less extent, imbibed from the Christian atmosphere in which they have been nurtured something of Christian feelings and principles. Even what good influence, then, that *commerce* may exert upon the heathen is traceable to Christianity; and thus, again, Christianity is seen to be the only hope of the present immense world of the heathen.

(4) But we have the positive evidence of the wonderful power of Christianity, in modern times, upon men plunged in the lowest depths of heathen ignorance and depravity. "Sixty years ago," says Anderson, in a late essay on Missions, "there was not a solitary native

Christian in Polynesia; now it would be difficult to find a professed idolater in the islands of Eastern or Central Polynesia, where Christian missionaries have been established. The hideous rites of their forefathers have ceased to be practiced. Their heathen legends and war-songs are forgotten; their cruel and desolating tribal wars, which were rapidly destroying the population, appear to be at an end. They are gathered together in peaceful village communities; they live under recognized codes of laws; they are constructing roads, cultivating their fertile lands, and engaging in commerce. On the return of the Sabbath, a very large proportion of the population attend the worship of God, and, in some instances, more than half the adult population are recognized members of Christian Churches. They educate their children, endeavoring to train them for usefulness in after-life. They sustain their native ministers, and send their noblest sons as missionaries to the heathen lands which lie farther west. There may not be the culture, the wealth, the refinement, of the older lands of Christendom. These things are the slow growth of ages; but these lands must no longer be regarded as a part of heathendom. In God's faithfulness and mercy, they have been won from the domains of heathendom, and have

been added to the domains of Christendom.*
Could any power on earth have so changed
those savage islanders except the gospel?
From being cannibals, in a few years they
have established all the forms and institutions
of civilized life. This great change could not
have been effected by any educational process.
To-day there are highly educated men in India,
but they are still heathen. Nana Sahib, one
of the leaders of the Sepoy rebellion, the author of the Cawnpore massacre, was a well-educated man, not only in his own language, but
also in English. His favorite poet was Lord
Byron. Yet he was truly a heathen. . . . No
religion refines and purifies as Christianity.
. . . But the most remarkable results of missionary labor are in the Fiji Islands. . . .
Thirty years ago they were all cannibals. A
more degraded race of men could not be found;
but in thirty years they have become a civilized Christian people. . . . Their language has
been mastered, school and religious books written, . . . and twenty-two thousand two hundred are members of the Church; the larger
part of the children are in the Sunday-school;
they have six hundred and sixty-three native
ministers, and more than one thousand school-teachers teach thirty-six thousand pupils in

---

* Report of London Missionary Society for 1866, p. 7.

their schools." These instances may suffice, without citing other remarkable instances—such as that of Madagascar, and other heathen lands. They are fully sufficient to prove that in modern times, as well as when in ancient days the gospel regenerated the heathen nations, Christianity has a power, never otherwise beheld, to elevate and purify the basest of mankind—a power superhuman and divine.

Thus the actual results of Christianity, attested both by the personal testimony of those who have practically tested her divine power, and by the great and permanent moral changes for the better apparent throughout her past history, and occurring also in our own day—results that no human wisdom or power has ever been able to effect, but which have, nevertheless, been wrought by Christianity, without the aid of human power—these also give incontrovertible evidence to the superiority of Christianity to all that is human, and assert that she is no less than divine.

CHAPTER IX.

THE WEIGHT OF THE EVIDENCE—RECAPITULATION AND CONCLUSION.

IN conclusion, let us now sum up the evidence that has been adduced, and estimate its weight. The question before us is whether or not Christianity is superhuman and divine. In its decision we have seen, first, that a divine revelation is possible; that human testimony is competent to prove it; and that the evidence in this particular case shows that the narrative of the facts, cited to prove it, must be accepted as authentic and true. We have next examined those facts, group by group, and from them endeavored to show the divinity of Christianity as displayed alike in the origin and divine character of its Founder, its own divine teaching, its miraculous attendant circumstances in both prophecies and miracles, and its superhuman and divine results. These, let it be noted, are all evidences of matters of fact. On the other hand, there is absolutely no rival system of moral truth that has, or pretends to have, any *evidence* whatever, of such matters of fact, to support its claim.

12*

There is, then, *no* positive evidence of *any* opposing system being true. There are only some objections against Christianity, and these are not founded upon any contradictory evidence relating to the facts essential to Christianity, but only upon certain *a priori* speculations, and theories, or alleged facts of physical science, etc., which, if true, are, at most, but doubtfully inconsistent themselves with the great *facts* of Christianity, and for whose truth it may confidently be asserted that there is not a tithe of the evidence that there is for the truth of the latter—and which, in fine, are altogether denied by some scientists of great authority, and maintained by others to be not inconsistent with Christianity.

But, to perceive the extreme absurdity of such objections, let us remember that, were there beyond question a set of facts proved, which were apparently wholly inconsistent with Christianity, we still, upon the principles of science itself, should not be justified therefore in rejecting Christianity, if Christianity also has uncontroverted evidence of its own to show that its claims are true, for both may be true. It is not unknown in the history of science that two facts, or two sets of facts, have been proved by equal evidence to exist, which at first seemed utterly inconsistent with each other. But the truly scientific course in such a case was not to reject either, but, ascribing the difficulty, where it belongs, to *our* weakness of reason, etc., to go patiently to work to discover their real relation and actual harmony. So we must do in the case of science and Christianity. Besides, on what principle are we authorized to reject one set of facts, if supported by proper evidence, in favor of another set, which also are supported only by evidence? If Christianity and science really do come in conflict, why not reject science if Christianity possesses sufficient evidence of its truth? Whether it has such sufficient evidence is indeed another question, and proper to be asked; but if it has, it is not to be then set aside because it is supposed to conflict with some other system which is itself established only because it too has sufficient evidence. In fine, the whole question is manifestly but a question of evidence. If there is not sufficient positive evidence for the establishment of Christianity, then we must reject it; if there is, we must, on *scientific* principles, admit its claims, though there even be (which, indeed, in the judgment of many of the best scientists, is very far from certain) some other facts undoubtedly proved which, to our imperfect minds, *seem* to be entirely inconsistent therewith.

The same difficulty continually occurs also in trials at law. Almost always, in the trial of causes, there are some circumstances proved which seem to be contradictory to the decision rendered. Nevertheless, a decision of some sort must be made; and it is properly thought, in such cases, that the circumstances which may apparently contradict what seems, upon the whole, to be the truth of the matter, are not really contradictory, but only, because of our want of full information, weakness of reason, etc., incapable of being harmonized by us.

Nay, in the commonest affairs of life—in those things which are most open to our inspection, most familiar to us, and therefore most likely to be understood—there exists, in very many cases, this apparent contradiction, unexplainable by us. Surely this should teach us humility, and lead us to beware of saying, in the higher and more difficult things of religion and science, because, in the judgment of some, though not of others, there exists an apparent inconsistency, that therefore Christianity must be rejected.

Christianity, then, must have its claims decided *independently*—just as those of science or any other system are—by the positive evidences it adduces for their establishment. Accordingly, to those evidences we confidently appeal, and assert that, upon all the settled rules of evidence, as quoted in Part First—rules which are always followed everywhere else, in common life, in trials at law, and in the researches of science, for the establishment of matters of fact—those evidences are overwhelmingly conclusive in its favor. For,

1st. Every kind of evidence possible in the nature of the case is presented in its favor. We should indeed demand that a religion professing to be divine should give some evidence of its divinity in—(1) The origin and (2) the character of its Founder; (3) his teaching; (4) his prophecies; (5) his miraculous works; (6) and in the actual results accomplished among men. But we can demand no other kind of evidence. But Christianity, and no other religion, has them all. What more can we ask?

2d. On the other hand, to disbelieve Christianity, we must believe—(1) That it arose, not as alleged (though its alleged origin is uncontradicted by any *evidence*), but in some other way, unknown and inconceivable, but yet sufficient to produce, what Christianity undoubtedly is, the purest and mightiest moral system that has ever existed on earth. (2) That the testimony of Christ and his apostles, though they are acknowledged to have been the wisest and best of men, was false, or that Christ never really existed, and those wonderful books of the Gospels which give an account of his life—impossible for merely human ability to produce at all—were forgeries and lies, and that when there was no worldly advantage to gain from the lie, but every thing to lose. (3) That vast numbers of people, including fierce and watchful enemies as well as friends, were deceived about frequent and public miracles, or, knowing their falsity, yet remained silent about them. (4) That the prophecies, extending through generations for their fulfillment, were but the result of human sagacity and penetration. (5) Finally, that all Christians have, in all succeeding ages, been mistaken as to their own experience, and have been miserably deluded, even to the endurance of torture and death, sooner than they would renounce their religion. Surely it requires more credulity to assent to the asseverations of infidelity than to believe in Christ.*

---

* THE UNBELIEVER'S CREED.—"1. I believe there is no God, but that matter is God, and God is matter, and that it is no matter whether there is any God or no. 2. I believe that the world was not made; that the world made itself; that it had no beginning, and that it will last forever, world without end. 3. I believe that man is a beast; that the soul is the body, and the body is the soul; and

3d. Finally, the full force of the argument is to be seen only when we consider not only the weight of the evidence, which each of the great facts adduced in support of Christianity carries, but their cumulative, overpowering weight when taken together. The improbability of Christianity's being false arises not merely from the improbability that any one of these remarkable characteristics should be found attending a false system, but from the almost infinite improbability that so many of those characteristics should so harmoniously *coincide* therein. It is a settled point in courts of law that, in the trial of causes, the decision should not be reached by the consideration of any single matter of fact, but by the consideration of all the issues in the case, and what upon the whole is established by the preponderating evidence. This principle is fully ad-

---

after death there is neither body nor soul. 4. I believe that there is no religion; that natural religion is the only religion; and that all religion is unnatural. 5. I believe not in Moses; I believe in the First Philosophy; I believe not the Evangelists; I believe in Chubb, Collins, Hume, Voltaire, and Tom Paine; I believe not St. Paul. 6. I believe not Revelation; I believe in the Talmud and the Koran; I believe not the Bible; I believe in Socrates; I believe in Confucius; I believe in Mohammed; I believe not in Christ. 7. Lastly, I believe in all unbelief." — *Horne's Introduction*, Vol. I., p. 159, Note 4.

mitted in the investigations of science also (*vide* Jevous's "Principles of Science," I., 239); and the rule which is there laid down to ascertain the probability of any conclusion is, to multiply together "the fractions expressing the probabilities of the premises," and the fraction resulting will express the probability of the whole taken together. For instance, if we have five facts concurring to establish a conclusion, and the probability of each of those supporting facts is as 5 to 1, or $\frac{5}{1}$, the probability of the conclusion, derived from the concurrence of those separate five probable facts, is found by multiplying the fraction $\frac{5}{1}$ by itself five times, amounting to $\frac{5625}{1}$, or as 5625 to 1. Now, applying this to ascertain the degree of probability of the divinity of the Scriptures, we get an almost infinite probability. Take, for example, the first set of facts adduced—viz., the preparation of the world for Christ's coming. Even infidels must admit, to account upon their own theories for the great and rapid spread of Christianity, that the world was ripe for his coming. They must also admit, seeing the utter final failure of all other would-be reformers, even such as Socrates, Plato, Confucius, or as Voltaire, Rousseau, etc.—whom some claim to be equal, or even superior, to Christ—that such an exceedingly favorable opportunity for reforming mankind but seldom occurs. We are authorized, then, in asserting that the improbability of such a concurrence of favorable circumstances happening to a merely human teacher, who could have no power of previously arranging them, is very great. Adding to this the prophecies that foretold so minutely the coming of Jesus, the improbability of the concurrence of a second such fortunate coincidence is made much greater, and, since this is the sole case of the kind in the history of the world, can be accounted as no less than many thousands to one — let us, however, with extreme reserve say, as 20 to 1, or $\frac{20}{1}$. Again, the improbability that such a Teacher should far surpass in character all others of the human race, is equal, at least, to the whole number of the human family to one—that is, some hundreds of thousands of millions to one—but still let us say this too is but as $\frac{20}{1}$. So, respectively, as to the superiority of his teaching far surpassing all that all others have taught; his wonderful works, esteemed by all that saw him as miracles; his predictions, and the amazing results of his mission—let us estimate the improbability of each occurring in a merely human system at the same ratio of $\frac{20}{1}$ (although since, in fact, the whole multitude of human systems—much more in number than 20 — from time to time propounded, have been, without exception, deficient in all these particulars, this is, without doubt, a ratio much too small), and multiply. The result is $\frac{32000000}{1}$, or it is 32,000,000 times to 1 improbable that these characteristics should concur in any merely human system; in other words, it is 32,000,000 times to 1 probable that Christianity is superhuman and divine. We believe this is much below the true probability. But if any one thinks this ratio of $\frac{20}{1}$ in each of the above cases is too great, let him put it at 5 to 1—nay, take even 2 to 1—and still, in the latter case, we shall have, as the probability of our conclusion, 32 to 1—a proportion which ought to satisfy every candid mind.

We conclude, then, our review with the full conviction that Christianity, beyond any reasonable doubt, is truly divine.

(FINISHED CHRISTMAS-DAY, 1879. LAUS DEO!)

www.ingramcontent.com/pod-product-compliance
Lightning Source LLC
Chambersburg PA
CBHW032119230426
43672CB00009B/1795